PURDUE UNIVERSITY'S
ROSS-ADE STADIUM

PURDUE UNIVERSITY'S
ROSS-ADE STADIUM
• 100 GREATEST GAMES •

CORY W. PALM

THE
History
PRESS

Published by The History Press
Charleston, SC
www.historypress.com

First published 2024

Manufactured in the United States

ISBN 9781467151382

Library of Congress Control Number: 2024937021

CONTENTS

CONTENTS

ACKNOWLEDGEMENTS

This project would not have been possible without the support of numerous individuals. First and foremost, thanks to the Strategic Communications staff at Purdue Athletics for the research and approval they provided for the better part of three years. Thanks are in order specifically to my great friend Matt Rector, who not only helped inspire the idea for this project but was also supportive at every step along the way. We miss you more than you would have ever imagined! Thanks to colleagues Marcia Iles, Rachel Coe and Matthew Staudt for listening and allowing me to bounce ideas around while working through the creative process. Endless gratitude goes out as well to John Rodrigue and the entire team at The History Press for seeing the diamond in what was a very rough idea.

This project could have never happened without a century's worth of wonderful journalism at local newspapers around the Midwest. What a wonderful thing it is to have that work at our fingertips in this digital age.

Finally, I can never express how grateful I am to my home team, Jaclyn and Alyssa. They deal with all of the trials and tribulations of my career in college athletics and somehow still find a way to love me. In you, God has blessed me beyond measure.

AUTHOR'S NOTE

There is no better way to learn the history of something than to read contemporary reports of the events that defined that entity. In that way, this text provides a wonderful history of Purdue Football in telling the story of the events that transpired inside the confines of Ross-Ade Stadium.

In the pages that follow, you'll see dozens of names you recognize, and you'll get a sense for exactly why they became legends. You'll read of moments in Purdue Football history with which you are familiar, and you'll hopefully learn of many more moments that you never knew about. No doubt many of these stories will only make your fondness for the Boilermakers grow stronger. Names like Kizer, McGannon, Butkovich, Mollenkopf, Phipps, Dierking, Young, Smith, Morales and Trent are worth remembering.

A few notes before you get started. The goal of this tome is not to tell you the history of Ross-Ade Stadium itself, although that story is also worth reading about. To do so, I would suggest *Ross-Ade: Their Stories, Stadium and Legacies* by Robert Kriebel.

You will notice that the list of "100 Greatest Games" skews much heavier toward the last four decades or so. I assure you this is not due to recency bias but rather because of the evolution of college football. It wasn't until 1965 that football schedules included more than nine games total, and for the first four decades of Ross-Ade's existence, the stadium hosted an average of four games per year rather than the seven or eight games per year that has become more common in recent years.

Finally, you'll notice that this list is laid out chronologically rather than as a ranked Top 100. There are myriad reasons for this, not the least of which is personal bias. To do a definitive list would be futile since it would likely skew to games that the person doing the ranking attended in person. One would need to determine what factors matter most and attempt to make a fair and unbiased system to assign value to each factor in order to get a list, which would almost assuredly draw opinion-based criticism by trying to justify opinions as definitive facts. Of course, I have my own personal Top 10 list of Ross-Ade's Greatest Games. Hopefully after reading this book, you will as well. To continue the conversation and to see my personal Top 10, join me on Twitter @RossAde100.

1920s
NEW BEGINNINGS

DAVID ROSS, GEORGE ADE AND JAMES PHELAN

November 22, 1924

Purdue 26, Indiana 7—First Game at Ross-Ade Stadium

In the history of Purdue Football, there is no rivalry more important than Indiana. It is only appropriate, then, that the first game in the history of Ross-Ade Stadium would be against the Hoosiers in the final game of the 1924 season. Two weeks earlier, Purdue had dispatched DePauw in the final game at Stuart Field, the university's home venue for more than three decades. That 36–0 win cleared the way for an epic celebration of the new home for the Boilermakers two weeks later.

With alumni in town from around the country to celebrate Homecoming as well as the dedication of the new monument to Purdue Football, the team did not disappoint. Indiana came into the contest riding a two-game winning streak and looking to secure a winning record for the season. The Boilermakers, in front of a very partisan crowd of more than twenty thousand people, had other ideas.

After the teams exchanged punts to start the game, the Boilermakers got on the board first. Taking over near midfield, back-to-back runs by Rudolph "Tudy" Bahr and Harold Harmeson earned first downs and took the ball to Indiana's 26-yard line. Purdue head coach Jimmy Phelan then unleashed some trickery as Harmeson took a pitch and swept to the right before stopping on a dime and flinging the ball back across the field to Bahr. The

University presidents Edward C. Elliott and William Lowe Bryant ceremoniously opened Ross-Ade Stadium on November 22, 1924. *Purdue Athletics.*

Rudolph "Tudy" Bahr scored the first touchdown in Ross-Ade Stadium history while leading the Boilermaker ground attack. *Purdue Athletics.*

entire Hoosier secondary had been fooled, and no one was within 15 yards of Bahr as he eased into the end zone untouched. Harmeson's PAT failed, but the Boilermakers led 6–0.

Indiana briefly took the lead in the second quarter on a short scoring run by Max Lorber, but just before halftime, the Boilermakers recaptured the lead for good. From near midfield, Bahr took the pitch and dropped back to pass, connecting with a streaking Harmeson who regained his footing after a brief stumble and barreled in for a 45-yard touchdown reception.

Bahr added a pair of rushing touchdowns in the second half, while the Purdue defense absolutely dominated the game, holding the Hoosiers without a first down after halftime. Offensively, Purdue outgained IU 311 yards to 88 yards for the game. The unsung hero for the Boilermakers may have been punter Bo Worth, who repeatedly won the field position battle for his team. On thirteen punts, Worth averaged better than 42 yards per punt, and the Hoosier offense was constantly starting in a bad spot.

As great as the victory was for Purdue players and fans alike, the ceremony surrounding the game was even more impressive. A twenty-one-gun artillery salute from Purdue ROTC members opened the dedication ceremonies. The All-American Marching Band, under the direction of Professor P.S. Emrick, played the national anthem while unfurling a giant American flag. David Ross and George Ade were presented gold medallions of appreciation by student body president E.C. Warrick. Just before the start of the game, a small plane decked out in black and gold flew just above the stadium and dropped the game ball. Among the dignitaries in attendance were both sitting U.S. senators from the state of Indiana, as well as a wide array of state officials including Governor-elect Edward Jackson. University presidents Edward C. Elliott and William Lowe Bryan were also on hand to dedicate the stadium.

At the alumni dinner in the Memorial Union after the game, George Ade perfectly captured the importance of the day. "My good friends, this is one of the days for which we have waited," the great playwright exclaimed to more than five hundred in attendance. "We are going to be respected, and feared, by our rivals more than ever before. From now on, when we talk about Purdue, we are going to have something to talk about."

NOVEMBER 20, 1926

PURDUE 24, INDIANA 14—HANGING THE FIRST "P" ON THE OLD OAKEN BUCKET

As the final day of the 1926 season dawned, the Boilermakers prepared once more for their biggest rival, the Indiana Hoosiers. This time, however, the Old Gold and Black were fighting for a bit more than pride. Although this was the twenty-ninth meeting between the two rivals, it was just the second time they'd be playing for the Old Oaken Bucket.

When the trophy debuted the year before in Bloomington, the game ended in a 0–0 tie, and an iron "I-P" became the first link in the chain hanging from the handle. Here now, one year later, was finally a chance to add a solitary "P."

Some fifteen thousand fans showed up to a frigid Ross-Ade Stadium for the final battle of the season. The field was frozen after winter's first snow had blanketed campus the day before. It wasn't just Purdue fans filling the stands, as an IU Special from Bloomington came up the Monon line that morning carrying hundreds of Crimson and Cream supporters along with the Hoosier band. Additional specials from points farther south swelled the

Opposite: The Old Oaken Bucket is presented before the 1926 game, won by the Boilermakers for the first time after the inaugural rivalry battle ended in a scoreless tie. *Purdue Athletics.*

Left: Chester "Cotton" Wilcox with the Old Oaken Bucket after the victorious "P" has been added. Wilcox led a strong Purdue rushing attack in the 26–14 win. *Purdue Athletics.*

Hoosier faithful to well over one thousand by the time they converged in West Lafayette.

The home team got on the board first as Chester "Cotton" Wilcox rambled 56 yards for a score midway through the opening stanza. L.C. Cook scored on a sweep around the left end early in the second quarter to extend the lead to 14–0. Indiana cut the lead in half with a score of its own, but Purdue's Bob Wilson booted a 40-yard drop kick through the uprights on the final play of the first half put the Boilermakers up 17–7 at the break.

IU took advantage of several Purdue penalties at the beginning of the third quarter and cut the lead to 17–14. On the next drive, Boilermaker fullback Dutch Koransky closed out the scoring after four straight plunges through the center of the line. After waiting out a scoreless fourth quarter, the home crowd officially celebrated the capturing of the Old Oaken Bucket for the first time.

The Boilermakers dominated the day rushing for 349 yards and totaling eighteen first downs on the afternoon. Purdue finished the season with a 5-2-1 record, 2-1-1 in conference and in third place. The Boilermakers won seven of the next eight games in the series and, as of 2023, have hung sixty-two "P" links on the chain to thirty-two "I" links.

NOVEMBER 24, 1928

PURDUE 14, INDIANA 0—PURDUE SHUTS OUT HOOSIERS

A record crowd of twenty-five thousand people packed Ross-Ade Stadium for the final game of the 1928 season as the Boilermakers once again welcomed the hated Hoosiers to town. What had been a promising season for Indiana had fallen apart with a three-game losing streak in the middle of the campaign, and now the team was just hoping to salvage something with a win over its rival. The Boilermakers, meanwhile, had lost heartbreakers to Northwestern and Minnesota but had tied a good Wisconsin team and shut out their other four opponents. Head Coach Jimmy Phelan came into the final game of the season looking to secure his third straight season with at least five victories.

The temperature was pleasant for the final Saturday in November, but a stiff wind out of the south would likely play a part in the game's outcome, as it would provide a distinct advantage to the team defending the south end zone.

The Boilermakers won the coin toss and chose to defend the north end zone to begin the game, giving IU the chance to take the ball. Anticipating a field position game and hoping to start things off on a good foot, Indiana elected to kick off rather than receiving the opening salvo. The Boilermakers rendered the point moot as they promptly drove downfield, only to see Glen Harmeson miss a field goal attempt. After the teams exchanged punts, the Hoosier offense drove to midfield. Indiana quarterback Paul Balay dropped back to pass and failed to see Purdue defensive back Ralph "Pest" Welch lurking in the background. Welch intercepted the throw and settled in behind a wall of blockers, crossing the goal line 65 yards later with the game's first score.

The Boilermakers clung to that 7–0 lead until early in the third quarter, when their offense finally strung together a drive. The home team received the ball to start the second half and drove 56 yards for its second score of the afternoon. Each member of the backfield contributed on the drive, but it was Welch who covered the final 7 yards to pay dirt.

Indiana's offense put together a few scoring threats in the second half, but the Boilermaker defense answered the call each time to preserve its fifth shutout victory of the season. The Hoosiers actually totaled more offense on the afternoon, but three turnovers and a blocked punt helped prove the difference.

Eleven seniors finished their Purdue playing careers that afternoon, going out as the most successful group to ever play for Purdue, compiling a record of 16-6-4 in their three years. But for those who remained on the roster, even better days were just around the corner.

OCTOBER 12, 1929

PURDUE 30, MICHIGAN 16—FURIOUS COMEBACK VS. WOLVERINES

Week one of the 1929 season saw Purdue defeat Kansas State 26–14 in a non-conference tune-up. In week two, the Boilermakers welcomed the Michigan Wolverines to town for the Big Ten opener. Michigan was riding high after three resounding wins to open the '29 campaign and was hoping to continue that dominance in its first road game.

The Boilermakers surprised the sold-out crowd of twenty-five thousand fans when they took the field in Old Gold jerseys instead of the traditional black tops they normally wore at home. It was a special look for what would end up being a very special day. The Boilermakers received the opening kick, but the game quickly settled into a field position battle, as was common for the era. Finally, late in the second quarter, Ralph "Pest" Welch burst through the center of the line and rumbled 35 yards to break the tie. Purdue missed the PAT but carried their 6–0 lead into halftime.

The second half shaped up to be nothing at all like the first as Michigan turned an early interception into 3 points. After going nowhere on the ensuing possession, Welch dropped back to punt. Michigan crashed through the line and blocked the effort, falling on the loose ball in the end zone. Suddenly the home team was trailing. Another Purdue possession went nowhere, and Michigan's offense finally got in on the scoring with a 14-yard touchdown run. The Wolverines found themselves up, 16–6.

It was shaping up to be an unmitigated disaster for the home team. Finally, late in the third quarter, the Boilermakers caught a break as Alex Yunevich

Alex Yunevich busts through the Michigan line on his way to the end zone for one of his three touchdowns in the upset. *Purdue Athletics.*

intercepted a Michigan pass. The offense went to work driving downfield, and on the first play of the final stanza, Yunevich crossed the goal line to cut into the Michigan lead. On Michigan's next possession, a new hero emerged. Michigan dropped back to punt, and Elmer Sleight broke through the line, blocking the kick and recovering the loose pigskin on the 5-yard line. Moments later, Yunevich scored again, and the home team retook the lead, 18–16, with five minutes to play.

The Boilermakers weren't done. On their next possession, Glen Harmeson scampered 30 yards before being brought down a yard shy of the goal line, setting up Yunevich's third scoring run of the day. Harmeson then had a 26-yard run to set up the final score of the day, an Elbert Caraway sweep that covered 30 yards and put the exclamation point on the victory. The Boilermakers had put up 24 points in the final quarter to defeat mighty Michigan, 30–16.

Yunevich, a sophomore playing in just his second game with the varsity eleven, was the breakout star with twenty-one rushes for 127 yards and three scores along with that key interception. Harmeson finished with 126 yards on twenty-one carries, while Welch logged 68 yards on the ground in thirteen attempts and one score. All told, the Boilermakers rushed for 357 yards and fourteen first downs as the front seven dominated. Elmer Sleight set himself apart with the blocked punt and several tackles for loss from his defensive tackle position.

It was one of the finest games in Purdue history and certainly the greatest contest in the first five years of Ross-Ade Stadium. For the 1929 Boilermaker team, it was just the beginning of a truly special season.

November 16, 1929

Purdue 7, Iowa 0—Boilermakers Clinch First Outright Big Ten Title

At the time, it was considered by many to be the most important game the Purdue football team had ever played. The undefeated Boilermakers welcomed the 4-1-1 Iowa Hawkeyes to Ross-Ade Stadium for the final home game of the 1929 season. Purdue had already dispatched Kansas State, Michigan, DePauw, Chicago, Wisconsin and Mississippi. A Homecoming win over the Hawkeyes would clinch a Big Ten title and move the team one game away from the program's first undefeated season since 1892.

Both teams settled into a defensive posture early, knowing full well that they were each facing one of the best defensive units in the nation. The Boilermakers had surrendered two touchdowns in their previous five games. The Hawkeyes, meanwhile, could boast an even better record, having given up just three touchdowns on the entire season.

As the second quarter began, Purdue had the ball at its own 41-yard line. A 2-yard dive by Alex Yunevich was followed by 5-yard run by Glen Harmeson. On third-and-3 from near midfield, Harmeson lofted a perfect pass to Bill Woerner for 28 yards down to the Iowa 25. Ralph "Pest" Welch

Left: Ralph "Pest" Welch led the Boilermakers to a perfect 1929 season, earning All-America honors in the process. *Purdue Athletics.*

Right: Glen Harmeson starred in his Senior Day contest against Iowa, helping Purdue to its first outright Big Ten title. *Purdue Athletics.*

gained 3, and after an Iowa timeout, Harmeson got 5 more yards down to the Iowa 18. Once again, a third-down pass play was called, and Harmeson again found Woerner, this time in the end zone, to break the deadlock. Harmeson banked his point-after attempt off the left upright and through for the extra point, and the Boilermakers had a 7–0 lead.

That score would be enough to win the day, as the Hawkeyes threatened a few times but were turned away by the stout Purdue defense on each occasion. In the end, the two offenses combined for just 412 yards. Purdue attempted just four passes on the day, and the only two completions came on the scoring drive. The defense caused three Iowa turnovers, gathering two interceptions and the game's only fumble.

When the dust settled, with the help of Indiana and Michigan taking care of Northwestern and Minnesota, respectively, the Boilermakers stood alone as Big Ten champions. They had shared a title in 1918 with a conference record of 1-0 (during a season dramatically affected by both World War I and the Spanish flu pandemic) but had never won a title outright.

In their final home game, seniors Glen Harmeson, Pest Welch and Elmer Sleight had played the perfect game. A week later, with a 32–0 win at Indiana, they wrapped up the perfect season. All three earned all-conference honors, while Sleight and Welch were also consensus All-Americans, becoming the first two All-Americans in school history.

1930s
CHAMPIONSHIP PEDIGREE

FROM NOBLE KIZER TO MAL ELWARD

OCTOBER 25, 1930

PURDUE 7, WISCONSIN 6—A GAME OF INCHES

More than twenty-eight thousand descended on West Lafayette for Homecoming 1930 to see their Boilermakers take on Wisconsin. They arrived via private airplane at the newly opened Purdue Airport across campus and caravans of cars from all around the state. Four specials came down the rails from Madison bringing two thousand Badger fans to town. The anticipation for the game was off the charts as 4-0 Wisconsin looked to stay in the hunt for a Big Ten title. What's more, in their four wins, the Badgers had surrendered just one touchdown total. Purdue came in 2-1, the only blemish a 14–13 loss at Michigan two weeks prior.

A sloppy first half saw each side trade fumbles and punts, with field position being of the utmost importance. Wisconsin caught the first real break with an interception late in the second quarter but ran out of time before they could capitalize, and the contest went to the break scoreless. The teams traded punts to start the third quarter as well, before the Boilermakers finally put together some offense.

Howard "Monk" Kissell got the drive started with a 16-yard gain out to midfield. After a first-down run by Roy Hortsmann went nowhere, halfback Ed Risk took a pitch and drifted back to pass. He saw Kissell running free and let fly with a perfect pass that hit his backfield mate in

A packed Ross-Ade Stadium was a common sight in the 1930s, with many fans taking advantage of the "bowl" nature of the stadium by standing at the outer edges. *Purdue Athletics.*

stride at the Wisconsin 20-yard line. Kissell covered the final 20 yards untouched, and the Boilermakers were on the board. It was the first points surrendered by the Badgers in more than twelve quarters of action. Lineman George VanBibber lined up to boot the PAT and sailed it through the goalposts perfectly.

Wisconsin wasn't done yet. With Purdue driving early in the fourth quarter, Wisconsin halfback Sammy Behr came up with a key interception in the end zone and returned it to the 10-yard line. Wisconsin got two consecutive first downs and then a 15-yard penalty on Purdue to move the ball to midfield. Behr then busted around the left end for a 30-yard gain, and the Badgers were threatening. Two plays later, Behr tossed a lateral to Ernie Lusby, who rumbled 16 yards to the two. A score seemed like a forgone conclusion, but someone forgot to tell the Boilermaker defensive line. Three straight plunges by the Badgers failed to reach the end zone. On fourth-and-goal, with the game on the line, Wisconsin changed tactics. Halfback Russ Rebholz took the snap, drifted to his right and lofted a pass over the Purdue defenders to Behr in the end zone. Wisconsin had marched 90 yards to pull within a point, 7–6. However, Rebholz's kick on the PAT went wide, and the Boilermakers held on to win, with the home crowd going wild.

Purdue would win their next three games as well, before falling to Indiana 7–6 in the season finale. The Boilermakers finished the season 6-2 and in third place in the conference. Ironically, both Boilermaker losses came by a single point because of missed PAT kicks of their own.

OCTOBER 3, 1931

PURDUE 28, WESTERN RESERVE 0; PURDUE 19, COE 0—LET'S PLAY TWO!

Opening day of the 1931 Purdue season was about as unique as they come, with not one but two different opponents coming to town the first weekend of October. Coach Noble Kizer knew that he had a good squad with great depth, so he split his team into two units and let each one play a game. It turned out, for all involved, that the plan worked just fine.

In game one of the doubleheader, the Boilermakers welcomed Western Reserve in a game slated to kick off at 1:00 p.m. Game two found Purdue taking on Coe College immediately after the conclusion of game one. When all was said and done, in eight quarters of football, the opponents had combined to score exactly zero points, and the record crowd of ten thousand fans went home happy, their team 2-0 on the year.

In game one, the Purdue roster was made up of sophomores and juniors, some seeing their first college varsity action. One player was seeing his first organized football action altogether. Sophomore Doxie Moore, a native of nearby Delphi, Indiana, who had come to Purdue to play basketball, scored three times for the Boilermakers.

In the night cap, senior fullback Alex Yunevich was the star, scoring all three Purdue touchdowns while amassing nearly 200 yards on just twelve carries. The Boilermakers jumped out to a 19–0 lead in the first half and then salted away the game in the final 30 minutes.

Purdue kept their season-opening shutout streak going the following week as well, handling Illinois 7–0. A tough road loss at Wisconsin in game four was the only blemish on the record as Kizer's squad closed out 1931 at 9-1, 5-1 in conference play, earning a share of the Big Ten title, the team's second in three seasons. They had one of the best defenses in the country, recording six shutouts on the year while giving up just 39 total points in ten games.

Following the season, that 1931 squad earned another prestigious honor, as football historian Parke Davis declared the Boilermakers national champions. It is, to date, the only national title won by Purdue in college football, as recognized by the NCAA.

OCTOBER 15, 1932

PURDUE 7, WISCONSIN 6—PARDONNER PROVIDES GAME-WINNING PAT

Wisconsin and Purdue were both predicted to be contenders for the Big Ten title when the 1932 season began, and the results of the first two weeks did nothing to dissuade anyone from that notion. The Badgers won their first two games over Marquette and Iowa, outscoring them 41–2 combined. The Boilermakers, meanwhile, also made quick work of Kansas State and Minnesota, setting up the Homecoming showdown with the team from Madison.

Perfect weather greeted a crowd of more than eighteen thousand to Ross-Ade, attendance seeing a bit of a drop-off as the nation crossed into year three of the Great Depression. One thing seemed certain: those in attendance were likely to see one heck of a game. The previous six match-ups between these teams had included two ties and a one-point Purdue win.

After a scoreless first quarter, the Boilermakers got something going early in the second. A ten-play, 65-yard drive was capped off by Roy Horstmann diving through the center of the line for the final yard. Paul Pardonner's drop kick was tipped but made its way through the goal posts anyway, and Purdue led 7–0. That's how it stayed until the closing seconds of the first half, when Wisconsin pulled out all the stops. On second down from the Purdue 42-yard line, halfback Joe Linfor took the snap and fired a pitch to fullback Harold Smith. Smith rolled out before launching a ball downfield to end George Thurner. As the Purdue defenders converged on Thurner, the Badger receiver jumped in the air and tossed a lateral to guard Milt Kummer, who grabbed the ball and rumbled the final 20 yards to pay dirt, untouched. However, just as had happened two years earlier, with a chance to tie the game, Wisconsin missed the PAT, and the score remained 7–6 in favor of the home team.

The second half saw both teams struggle to move the ball, with each side getting turned away by the opposing defense. In the end, the two second quarter touchdowns accounted for all of the day's scoring, and the

Boilermakers once again triumphed because of a missed PAT. Wisconsin would win four of their final five games and earn a 7–7 tie at Ohio State to finish the year 6-1-1. Purdue, meanwhile, would push toward its second consecutive Big Ten title.

November 19, 1932

Purdue 25, Indiana 7—Boilermakers Win Bucket, Clinch Title

More than twenty-two thousand fans poured into Ross-Ade Stadium for the final game of the 1932 season, hoping to witness their beloved Boilermakers clinch the conference crown. What a year it had been for Purdue Athletics! In March, Johnny Wooden had earned National Player of the Year honors while leading the basketball team to a 17-1 record and the Big Ten title, giving Piggy Lambert his sixth conference crown and, eventually, the Helms Foundation's National Championship honor as well. Now Purdue faithful were hoping to add another football championship to the list.

The game itself didn't offer much in the way of drama as the Boilermakers outclassed Indiana in nearly every facet of the contest. Paul Moss was the star of the day for the Boilermakers. The senior end, playing in his final game for the Old Gold and Black, had perhaps the finest performance of his career with five receptions for 169 yards and two scores. Each of the touchdowns Moss corralled went for 60-plus yards. After the season, he was selected as a unanimous All-American.

Moss's classmate and fellow All-American Roy Horstmann also scored in his final game for the Boilermakers, getting the home team on the board in the first quarter with a 3-yard plunge. The Boilermakers had run the score to 25–0 by midway through the third quarter when Head Coach Noble Kizer decided that the boys from Bloomington had had enough. The Boilermakers emptied the bench, and by the time IU finally put points on the board, it was against the Purdue third-string.

The 25–7 final secured the Old Oaken Bucket and locked up the conference title. Purdue finished the season 7-0-1, with a 7–7 tie at Northwestern being the only blemish on the ledger. The Boilermakers shared the conference title with undefeated national champion Michigan. It was the third Big Ten title in four seasons for the Boilermakers dating back to 1929 and capped off the first true golden era of Purdue Athletics.

NOVEMBER 16, 1935

PURDUE 12, IOWA 6—McGANNON LEADS DEFENSIVE WIN WITH PICK-SIX

The 1935 season started out with great promise for the Boilermakers. They'd won five of the final six games in 1934 and started with three straight victories in '35. The wheels came off quickly with three straight losses, and when Iowa came to town for the final home game of the season, there was little left to play for beyond pride. To make matters worse, emerging star halfback Cecil Isbell was questionable with an ankle injury.

When game time rolled around, Isbell hobbled out onto the field. He got the Boilermakers on the board with a touchdown pass to Frank Loebs early in the second quarter, and the Boilermakers took a 6–0 lead into the half. Two plays into the third quarter, Iowa responded with a touchdown pass of its own to knot the score at 6–6. The Hawkeyes continued to press their success through the air, and it would come back to bite them. Late in the third, Boilermaker defensive back Tom McGannon got a good read on a pass play and stepped in front of the Hawkeye receiver at the Purdue 32-yard line.

The Boilermakers instantly flipped the switch, as McGannon headed toward the opposite goal line, several teammates throwing key blocks to spring the 68-yard return on the pick-six. That play proved to be the difference, as Purdue closed out the 12–6 win. Purdue held the Hawks to just 52 yards rushing on the game, and although Iowa had more success through the air, the defense also came up with seven turnovers, including the game-deciding interception.

The Boilermakers closed out the season a week later with a 7–0 loss at Indiana to finish 4-4 on the year, and although it may have been a disappointment considering how the year at started, it was also the tenth straight season the team finished with a record at or above .500, a feat only matched one other time in program history.

November 21, 1936

Purdue 20, Indiana 20—Isbell Shines in Explosive Second Half

Gray skies and a brisk wind out of the west greeted the record crowd of more than thirty thousand to Ross-Ade for the 1936 Old Oaken Bucket game. A great game was expected between two teams with identical 5-2 records. Fans were still settling into their seats when Indiana's Vernon Huffman returned the opening kickoff 90 yards to the 10-yard line. The Hoosiers advanced to the Purdue 1-yard line but turned the ball over on downs as the Boilermaker defense stiffened. The teams traded punts the rest of the half and went to the locker room scoreless.

The Boilermakers seized control of the game in the third quarter with a pair of Cecil Isbell touchdown passes. Isbell converted both PATs, although one was nullified due to a holding call on the front line, and the lead stood at 13–0. Then Huffman brought the Hoosier offense to life, reeling off 20 unanswered points and taking the lead with just minutes remaining in the game. The Boilermakers took over at their own 23-yard line, desperately needing a touchdown. Isbell hit Powell on first down for 18 yards. Cecil then connected with a diving Red Zachary on the next play for a 25-yard gain to the Hoosier 30. John Drake caught Isbell's next pass for 15 yards. Two plays later, Isbell connected with Zachary for his third passing touchdown of the half, bringing the Boilermakers to within a point, 20–19. The delirious crowd immediately caught themselves, and a hush fell over the stadium, as the home team was still a kick away from tying the game. Team captain George Bell snapped the ball, Drake grabbed it and held it in place and Cecil connected on a perfect PAT to tie the score at 20. One minute later the final gun sounded, bringing the great contest to a close.

The Boilermakers finished the season at 5-2-1, a great year by any measure but even more so after the tragic way it began. During the team's preseason training camp, a drain pipe in the showers got clogged, causing water to rise in the shower room. On top of the water was a layer of gasoline, commonly used to remove tape adhesive at the time. As the water rose, fumes reached the hot water tank in the corner of the room and ignited. Fire swept through the shower room, killing players Carl Dahlbeck and Tom McGannon, hero of the 1935 win over Iowa, and severely injuring several others.

One of those badly burned was a fullback named Lowell Decker. After ten weeks in a Lafayette hospital, Decker was discharged on the day of the

Tom McGannon (no. 22 on the far left) was the star of the 1935 win over Iowa. Nine months later, he would fall victim to one of the worst tragedies in program history. *Purdue Athletics.*

Bucket game. He insisted on being on the sideline with his team. The junior from Reading, Michigan, sat in a car inside the stadium, very near to the Purdue bench. When the game was over, Decker's teammates secured the game ball and presented it to him.

One other note on the 1936 Bucket game: it would be the final game on the sidelines for Hall of Fame coach Noble Kizer. In the summer of 1937, Kizer was struck with a kidney ailment and had to take a leave from his duties as head coach. He never returned to the sideline, retiring with a 42-13-3 record in his seven years at the helm, winning two Big Ten titles and never finishing worse than fourth in the league. Kizer remained Purdue's athletics director.

October 9, 1937

Purdue 7, Carnegie Tech 0—Defense Stands Tall on Homecoming

A steady morning rain greeted Purdue fans hoping to take in the 1937 Homecoming battle with Carnegie Tech, a burgeoning rival from Pittsburgh. It would be the sixth showdown of the decade between the two engineering schools. The rain had not subsided by kickoff and kept the crowd small. But those who came were rewarded.

Neither team did much in the opening two quarters and entered halftime scoreless. In the third quarter, the Boilermakers got all the offense they needed on the afternoon when sophomore halfback Lou Brock sprinted

27 yards down the sideline, breaking a half dozen tackles on his way to the end zone. Isbell booted the extra point through the uprights, and the Boilermakers led 7–0.

Carnegie had a few chances to score but came up empty each time. Midway through the fourth quarter, the visitors caught a break on a pass interference call that gave them a first down at the Purdue 4-yard line. On four straight snaps, Carnegie Tech attempted a straight-ahead dive, trying to get the tying score. And on four straight plays, the Boilermaker eleven stood firm and protected their goal line. It was as close as the visitors would come the rest of the day, as the Boilermakers secured the 7–0 shutout and sent the fifteen thousand fans in attendance home happy.

The Boilermakers, under first-year head coach Mal Elward, finished the season 4-3-1, 2-2-1 in conference play. Elward had taken over the squad just before the season when Noble Kizer had to step away for medical reasons. Elward's boys fell into a pattern of winning a game and then losing a game all year long. But they won the all-important final game, securing the Old Oaken Bucket in Bloomington over a ranked Indiana team. And they saw the truth in the old adage that, sometimes, winning that game is enough.

October 22, 1938

Purdue 13, Wisconsin 7—Byelene Becomes Big Man on Campus

Homecoming 1938 saw the Boilermakers play host to the Wisconsin Badgers in a showdown between two very evenly matched teams. The Badgers were headed up by Harry Stuhldreher, formerly one of the famed "Four Horsemen" during his playing days at Notre Dame, now in his third season in Madison. They brought a 2-1 record to Ross-Ade that day to face the 2-1-1 Boilermaker squad.

The Badgers caught the first break late in the opening stanza when Lou Brock, star halfback for the Old Gold and Black, dropped back to field a punt. The kick initially went over his head, but Brock attempted to grab it anyway and promptly fumbled. Wisconsin took over at the Purdue 11-yard line and found themselves in the end zone in short order. The Badgers took a 7–0 lead into intermission but seemed to be in firm control. The Boilermakers had gained just 5 total yards in the opening thirty minutes and gained just one first down—by way of penalty.

But a different team emerged in the second half, quite literally. Sophomore halfback Mike Byelene replaced Brock in the backfield and sparked an offensive surge. Leading the Boilermakers down the field on the ground, Byelene dropped back and flung a pass to end Jack Krause for a 19-yard score to knot the game at 7–7.

Midway through the fourth quarter, the game still tied, Byelene once again played the hero. Purdue took over after a punt and on second-and-11 from their own 26-yard line, Byelene took a handoff toward left tackle. He slipped to his right as a teammate leveled a Wisconsin linebacker, and then he veered back to the left and saw the entire world open up before his eyes. He covered those 74 yards in an instant, crossing the goal line with the game-winning touchdown. Just that quickly, after replacing his All-Big Ten teammate in the backfield, one of the smallest men on the team became the big man on campus.

November 19, 1938

Purdue 13, Indiana 6—Record Crowd Sees Thriller

A picture-perfect day greeted the record crowd of more than thirty-two thousand fans to Ross-Ade Stadium on the final day of the 1938 season. With cloudless blue skies and unseasonably moderate temperatures, all was well with the world. It got even better for the home fans on the opening kickoff as Jack Brown caught the ball at his own 2-yard line and promptly sprinted 98 yards for a touchdown. Backfield mate Lou Brock booted the extra point, and the Boilermakers led 7–0 just seconds into the contest.

Indiana hoped to respond immediately, but on their third offensive snap, disaster struck. The Hoosiers fumbled, and Purdue linebacker Tony Ippolito appeared to scoop it up and scamper 31 yards for a score. However, the officials ruled the Boilermaker down, and the Hoosiers were given a reprieve. The score remained 7–0 for the rest of the half. The Hoosiers came out in the second half and had three successful run plays to get the ball to midfield before fumbling once more, this time seeing Big Joe Mihal cause and recover a turnover.

Brock and Brown did the rest of the work, covering the 43 yards on the ground, with the former finishing things off from 8 yards out. His kick was blocked, so the score stayed 13–0. Indiana got on the scoreboard in the fourth quarter but could do no further damage, with the home team taking the final 13–6. Fans went away happy with the win, which felt even more dominant than the final score considering the Boilermakers had seen four touchdowns called back for various reasons.

One of the best scenes of the day didn't happen anywhere near the field. Up in the press box, just prior to kickoff, Athletics Director Noble Kizer appeared. Kizer had resigned as head coach in the summer of 1937 and was just now making his way back to the stadium for the first time to see his boys play. Reporters, radio broadcasters and university officials gave Kizer a rousing welcome and a sustained round of applause to mark the occasion. Kizer would continue to battle a kidney ailment until his death in June 1940 at the age of forty.

1940s
THE WAR YEARS

BUTKOVICH, ISBELL AND DEMOSS

OCTOBER 25, 1941

PURDUE 7, IOWA 6—A TALE OF TWO KICKS

The 1941 Homecoming contest with the Iowa Hawkeyes was a tough one for Purdue fans to witness. For fifty minutes, they saw their team dominate everywhere but the scoreboard. And when the Hawkeyes got their only break of the game, a blocked punt late in the third quarter that they recovered for a touchdown, the home team trailed 6–0. Luckily, the Hawkeyes missed the PAT in what would prove to be a critical mistake by the visitors.

The Purdue offense got the ball with just under six minutes remaining in the game and finally put together a complete drive. A trio of sophomore backs—Johnny Andretich, Bob Chester and Francis Meakim—did the bulk of the work, with Andretich crashing over the goal line to knot the game at 6–6. Senior fullback John Petty trotted onto the field to attempt the PAT. Bob Johnson snapped the ball to quarterback Fred Smerke, who grabbed it and set it in place. Petty approached and connected with his big right foot, and the ball sailed perfectly down the middle to give the Boilermakers their Homecoming triumph.

On the day, Purdue outgained Iowa 249 yards to 89 yards offensively. The Boilermakers earned fifteen first downs to Iowa's three. But in the end, a single point separated the two conference rivals. It would be the final win of the year for Purdue, as they fell the next week at Fordham, tied Michigan State and lost road contests at Wisconsin and Indiana. In fact, Petty's extra point was the final point of the year, as the team was shut out in its final four contests. As fate would have it, the win over Iowa was the final victory for Head Coach Mal Elward. The Japanese attacked Pearl Harbor six weeks later, and Elward answered the call of his nation, returning to the U.S. Navy, with which he had served during World War I.

OCTOBER 2, 1943

PURDUE 40, ILLINOIS 21—BUTKOVICH BLASTS FORMER MATES

The 1943 Boilermaker squad was unlike any Purdue team in history. In the midst of World War II, the roster primarily comprised Navy and Marine Corps officer trainees from the Navy's V-12 training program. There were players from Missouri and Iowa, Fordham and Tulane. The school with the largest share of former players on the transient Boilermaker squad was the University of Illinois. Twelve Fighting Illini players dressed up for the Old Gold and Black in 1943, including six starters. None had a more profound impact on the Purdue squad than fullback Tony Butkovich.

Touchdown Tony set a conference scoring record and earned All-America honors that season thanks to a string of standout performances. His game against his former team is still counted among the greatest Boilermaker performances ever. After a sloppy first quarter that saw both teams struggle to hold on to the ball, Butkovich broke out. He opened the second stanza with a 3-yard scoring plunge to give the Boilermakers a 14–0 lead. Midway through the quarter, Butkovich took a pitch 80 yards for his second score of the afternoon, running the lead to 21–0. He scored again in the third quarter to extend the lead to 34–7.

The game well in hand, Head Coach Elmer Burnham sent in his reserves, and Butkovich and fellow former Illinois players Alex Agase and John Genis made their way over to the visiting sidelines to spend a little time with their former mates. They were able to hang out on the Illinois sideline right up until the Fighting Illini scored two quick touchdowns, making the score 34–21 with six minutes to go. Coach Burnham hollered across the field at his Purdue-Illini players and told them to come back to the home side, as he was putting the starters back into the game.

All-American fullback Tony Butkovich (no. 25 in the middle of the T-formation) was never more unstoppable than in the 1943 game against his former mates, the University of Illinois. *Purdue Athletics Film Archives.*

A big kickoff return by Sam Vacanti (a former Hawkeye), set up Butkovich's fourth score of the day. Touchdown Tony took the handoff from Vacanti and swept left, breaking four tackles on the way to the end zone, a 25-yard scamper and the final nail in the coffin as the Boilermakers won 40–21. For the day, Butkovich finished with a school-record 207 yards on just twelve carries, an average of 17.3 yards per carry, to go with his four scores. The highlight of Tony's day may have been when his little brother Bill, a freshman back for the Illini, brought him to the ground after a long gain.

After the game, Illinois head coach Ray Eliot spent a few minutes in the Purdue locker room, congratulating his former players on a fine performance. Butkovich stood there with a giant grin on his face, cradling the game ball tight. The Boilermakers went on to finish the 1943 season undefeated, the only major college football team to do so, although they would end up fourth in the final AP poll. Butkovich, Agase and several other marines would actually ship off to Parris Island with two game left in the season. Several saw action in the Pacific Theater, including Touchdown Tony Butkovich, who was killed on April 18, 1945, in the Battle of Okinawa.

September 22, 1945

Purdue 14, Marquette 13—Early Lead Holds Up

A driving rain greeted the 1945 opening day crowd of just over eleven thousand fans to Ross-Ade Stadium for what ended up being a much more thrilling game than anyone had bargained for. The first half saw the home team dominate in every facet, scoring a pair of touchdowns to take a 14–0 lead into halftime. The Boilermaker defense outperformed the offense, giving up just 10 yards to Marquette while not surrendering a single first down.

The Boilermakers got on the board thanks to a pair of freshmen, Bob DeMoss and David Shaw. DeMoss finished off a 59-yard scoring in the first quarter with a quarterback sneak to get the Boilermakers on the board. Early in the second quarter, Shaw broke loose for a 41-yard scoring run. All-American tackle Tom Hughes booted home both PATs to finish off each drive.

After a scoreless third quarter, Marquette's offense finally came to life. Five minutes into the final frame, the Hilltoppers used a few big plays to finally get on the scoreboard. A missed PAT left the score 14–6 in favor of the home team. The teams traded turnovers before Purdue punted away to give Marquette one last chance. The visitors, facing a fourth-and-6 from the Purdue 11-yard line, hit pay dirt once more to make it 14–12. The front wall blocked the point-after attempt, but Marquette scooped the ball up and crossed the goal line to earn the day's final point. The two-point conversion was still more than a decade away from being introduced to college football, so the Boilermakers' 14–13 victory was ensured.

On the day, Shaw made the most of his first career start, going for 115 yards on sixteen carries while also pulling double duty as Purdue's punter. Both he and DeMoss played the full sixty minutes in their debuts.

October 4, 1947

Purdue 24, Ohio State 20—Szulborski Carries Boilermakers

Heading into week two of the 1947 season, the Boilermakers had fallen on hard times. The last time the club won a conference game was nearly two years earlier, a 35–13 upset of no. 4 Ohio State in Columbus on October 20, 1945. The Old Gold and Black were 0-9-1 since in Big Ten play and not expected by many to change those fortunes soon. Purdue got on the board with a 63-yard scoring drive capped off by a touchdown pass from Bob DeMoss to Bob Heck. The joy of the thirty-four thousand home fans was short-lived, as Buckeye star Dean Sensabaugher took the ensuing kickoff 98 yards to tie the game, 7–7.

Penalties marred the rest of the first half, ending two Purdue scoring chances. They were able to add a 26-yard field goal and took a 10–7 lead into the half. On the second play of the second half, Sensabaugher scored on a brilliant 62-yard run, and the Buckeyes went on top 13–10. The home team responded with a sixteen-play, 78-yard scoring drive capped off with a 1-yard dive by halfback Norb Adams on fourth-and-goal. The Buckeyes answered with an eleven-play drive for a touchdown that swung the pendulum back in their favor, taking a 20–17 lead early in the fourth quarter.

The teams traded punts before the Boilermakers put together the game-winning drive. A 47-yard run by halfback Dick Bushnell and a steady diet of Harry "The Hurricane" Szulborski paced the attack. DeMoss scored on a quarterback sneak from a yard out for the game winner. Although his teammates got the glory of scoring Purdue's three touchdowns, Szulborski turned in one of the greatest performances in Purdue history. On the day, he had twenty-three carries for 172 yards while also contributing several nice punt returns. It wouldn't be the last time the diminutive halfback from Detroit made his mark in Ross-Ade.

October 25, 1947

Purdue 14, No. 5 Illinois 7—DeMoss Connects in Upset of Illini

The Illinois football team came into Ross-Ade Stadium in late October 1947 as the no. 5 team in the nation, its only blemish a tie on the road against fellow top-five ranked Army. The Boilermakers, meanwhile, stood at 2-2 on the season after wins over Ohio State and Boston University.

The Boilermakers got on the board first with a quick scoring drive midway through the first quarter, with fullback Jack Milito scoring from a yard out. The Illini pulled even late in the second with Chick Maggioli catching a pass from Perry Moss for the tying score. The big play on the drive was a pass from Moss to former Boilermaker Joe Buscemi for 24 yards, who had played for Purdue in 1943 as a Navy V-12 officer trainee.

By the late 1940s, capacity in Ross-Ade Stadium had risen to more than fifty-one thousand, thanks to permanent steel bleachers on the west side of the stadium. *Purdue Athletics.*

The Fighting Illini missed a field goal to open the third quarter, followed by the two teams trading punts. Another punt by George Papach pinned the Fighting Illini deep, rolling out of bounds at the 2-yard line. The visitors tried to flip the field position by punting on first down, but the boot didn't have the desired effect, going only to the Illinois 34 before coming to a rest. On first down, Bob DeMoss and Norb Adams connected for a 28-yard pass. On the next play, DeMoss faked a handoff and fired a bullet to Bob Heck in the end zone for the go-ahead score.

Early in the fourth quarter, the Fighting Illini drove inside the Purdue 20-yard line but fumbled away their last, best scoring chance, and the home team secured the upset. Illinois had the superior day in virtually every statistical category. They ran twenty-five more plays than Purdue, gained 70 more total yards and earned eleven more first downs. The Fighting Illini ran for more yards, threw for more yards and had fewer penalties. But in the only column that truly mattered, the final score, Purdue had the edge, 14–7. And for the forty-two thousand fans in attendance that afternoon, that was just fine.

1950s

A NEW IDENTITY

HOLCOMB, SAMUELS AND MOLLENKOPF

October 6, 1951

Purdue 34, Iowa 30—Samuels Leads Miracle Comeback

The 1951 Big Ten opener was expected to be a good game. By the end of the rainy afternoon in West Lafayette, many of the twenty-five thousand fans in attendance would be calling it the greatest game they'd ever seen. Iowa sophomore George Rice took the opening kickoff 101 yards for a touchdown to put the Hawks into the lead. They extended it to 13–0 early in the second quarter on another long score by Rice.

The Boilermakers finally got on the board a few minutes later when Phil Mateja returned a punt 92 yards to pay dirt to make it 13–7. Rice responded on Iowa's first offensive play with a 69-yard scoring run to make it 20–7. The Purdue offense came right back with a 90-yard scoring drive, capped off by a 15-yard run by fullback Jerry Thorpe. The home team added another score in the final minute of the first half on a quarterback sneak by Dale Samuels, and after a thrilling first thirty minutes, the score was tied 20–20.

The third quarter produced just a single field goal for Iowa, and they carried a slim lead into the final stanza. Midway through the fourth, Samuels was intercepted, and the Hawkeyes scored quickly, taking a 10-point lead. A seemingly insurmountable task ahead of them, the Purdue offense got to work, driving 70 yards in under four minutes. Samuels hit Phil Klezek on a screen pass for a score, cutting the lead to 30–27. The defense forced an

Quarterback Dale Samuels (no. 10 under center) lines up for a sneak to tie the game at 20–20 just before halftime. *Purdue Athletics Film Archives.*

Iowa punt, and the Boilers got the ball back with 1:30 remaining, 48 yards from the end zone.

First down brought an incomplete pass, and on second down, Roy Evans swept right for 10 yards and a fresh set of downs. More importantly, Evans made it out of bounds, stopping the clock. Tom Redinger lined up wide to the left and, at the snap of the ball, worked to get free of his coverage. Samuels dropped back to pass and let fly with a beauty that Redinger hauled in, scampering to the end zone. The Boilermakers had scored 14 points in the final four minutes to take a lead for the first time all afternoon. Iowa's last-gasp efforts at a miracle ended on a Purdue sack, the clock running out before the offense could get off a final snap.

The Boilermakers finished the year 5-4 overall but went 4-1 in conference play and placed second in the final standings. More importantly, they had tasted success that would lead to even better things in 1952.

NOVEMBER 22, 1952

PURDUE 21, INDIANA 16—A COMEBACK, A CHAMPIONSHIP AND A VOTE

The 1952 season finale set up perfectly for the Boilermakers. Although the overall record wasn't stellar at 3-3-2, Purdue was 3-1-1 in Big Ten play and trailed Michigan and Wisconsin by just a half game. A win on the season's final day could clinch the program's fourth Big Ten title and the first since the conference signed an agreement to send its champion to the Rose Bowl.

A chilly, rainy afternoon in Ross-Ade Stadium greeted forty thousand fans, and they saw the home team get out to an early lead. The Boilermakers took advantage of mistakes by the Hoosiers and led 14–0 at the end of the first quarter. The visitors rallied in the second quarter with their own pair of touchdowns, and at the break, the score stood at 14–14. Disaster struck for Purdue in the third quarter as Dale Samuels, in the shadow of his own goal line, fumbled a handoff to fullback Max Schmaling. Schmaling jumped on the loose ball, but the damage was done, as he was down in the end zone for an Indiana safety. The heavily favored home team headed to the fourth quarter trailing 16–14.

With the wind in their face and field turning into a sloppy mess, the Boilermakers had the odds against them. The home crowd got a charge of energy when the public address announcer gave the result from Columbus, Ohio. The Buckeyes had defeated Michigan 27–7, eliminating them from the conference title race. The team fed off that energy and put together the best offensive drive of the day, covering 66 yards, mostly on the ground. On third-and-3 from the 21-yard line with less than five minutes remaining, sophomore halfback Rex Brock slipped through a hole on the middle of the line and then cut outside. Brock followed the block of right tackle Ken Panfil to daylight, then the goal line and then everlasting glory.

The 21–16 final kept the Old Oaken Bucket in West Lafayette and the Boilermakers in contention for the conference crown. When word reached campus that Minnesota had scored late to tie Wisconsin 21–21, the Boilermakers had even more to celebrate: their first conference title since 1943.

With two teams tied for the title and no head-to-head tiebreaker, the conference's representative at the Rose Bowl was left up to a vote of the Big Ten's 10 athletics directors. The sole qualifier was to pick which team would best represent the Big Ten in the Rose Bowl. Commissioner Tug Wilson announced the results of the secret ballot on the following Monday, and the Badgers were picked to go to their first Rose Bowl—no further explanation given. Purdue fans would have to wait another fourteen years before getting their chance to go to Pasadena.

OCTOBER 3, 1953

PURDUE 6, NO. 1 MICHIGAN STATE 0—UPSET FOR THE AGES

Michigan State didn't join the Big Ten until the 1953 season, but by then, they already had a pretty well-established history with the Boilermakers. The teams had played seven previous times and knew each other fairly well. In 1952, the Spartans had beaten the Boilermakers 14–7 on the way to the national title. When the teams met in 1953, MSU was still atop the national standings, but Purdue had fallen off quite a bit from their Big Ten championship of the previous fall.

The Boilermakers had dropped their first four games of the '53 campaign. Things didn't look to get any better with no. 1 Michigan State and no. 4 Illinois next up on the docket. The Spartans brought to town a twenty-eight-game winning streak. They hadn't lost a contest since early in the 1950 season, and it was the only blemish in a three-year span. Hall of Fame coach Biggie Munn had things humming in East Lansing. But on this late October afternoon in West Lafayette, nothing went right for the Green and White.

The All-American Marching Band was on hand for one of the greatest upsets in school history when Purdue took down Big Ten newcomer no. 1 Michigan State in 1953. *Purdue Athletics.*

The two teams battled in a scoreless deadlock for three quarters, neither able to get an edge. Finally, Purdue broke through early in the fourth. On a drive that was extended thanks to a roughing the punter penalty against Michigan State, the Boilermakers kept things on the ground. Running backs Rex Brock, Dan Pobojewski and Ed "Bino" Neves took turns pushing the ball up the field. On fourth-and-goal from the 1, Pobojewski crashed in over left tackle. The PAT was missed, but the home team was on top 6–0.

There was high drama on the ensuing kickoff, as Leroy Bolden caught the kick and went 95 yards untouched for what looked like a back-breaking response. The play was called back, however, thanks to a clipping call against the Spartans. MSU gained only one first down in the remainder of the game, and the Boilermakers secured the upset.

It was a defensive masterpiece for Purdue as they held Michigan State to fewer than 200 yards of total offense while forcing six turnovers. Michigan State gained just seven first downs on the day.

The celebration on campus lasted through the night on Saturday as students rushed the field, tore down the goal posts and then paraded them all over town. It continued all day Sunday as fans continued their victory parades and revelries. It culminated with a pep rally Monday afternoon, with seven thousand people packing the Purdue Hall of Music and celebrating the team with songs, speeches and cheers.

MSU won the rest of their games, including the Rose Bowl after clinching the Big Ten title in their inaugural year. The Boilermakers lost their next three before closing the season out with a 30–0 win over Indiana to retain the Old Oaken Bucket for the sixth straight year. But for one glorious afternoon, the Boilermakers came to play and took down mighty Michigan State.

October 9, 1954

No. 5 Purdue 13, No. 6 Duke 13—Epic Battle for Two Future Hall of Famers

In a game that featured two future Pro Football Hall of Fame quarterbacks, naturally it was the run game that the Boilermakers relied on for a furious comeback when the Duke Blue Devils came to town in early October 1954. Fresh off a stunning upset at top-ranked Notre Dame the previous week, the Boilermakers had risen all the way to fifth in the Associated Press Poll. Duke

Future team captains Lamar Lundy (no. 81), Bob Clasey (no. 50) and Len Dawson (no. 16) were inches away from a program-defining win over no. 5 Duke in 1954. *Purdue Athletics.*

opened the season with wins over Penn and Tennessee and came into the game ranked sixth.

Sophomore second-string quarterback Sonny Jurgensen got the visitors on the board early in the second quarter, leading the Blue Devils to a scoring drive after a Purdue fumble. Jurgensen kicked the PAT, and Duke led 7–0. Starting QB Jerry Barger added a second score late in the half, and the Devils led 13–0 at the break. More than forty-seven thousand anxious fans watched the Band Day halftime show featuring thousands of marchers from around the state, hoping that Head Coach Stu Holcomb could figure out some way to get the home team on the board.

They didn't have to wait long for an answer, as the Boilermakers took their first possession of the second half 95 yards on eighteen plays, with backup QB Froncie Gutman diving over the goal line for the score. Jim Reichert missed the PAT, and the Duke lead stood at 13–6. The Blue Devils ran just three offensive plays before needing to punt, and starting signal caller Len Dawson trotted back onto the field.

Dawson engineered a 48-yard drive that took the rest of the third quarter and ended when Bill Murakowski crashed over the goal line on the first play of the fourth quarter. Dawson handled the now-vital point-after kick this time and converted, tying the game at 13–13 with one quarter to play.

Duke's only fourth-quarter threat came midway through the quarter when Jurgensen led the attack into Purdue territory, reaching the 21-yardline before stalling. A fake field goal didn't fool the Purdue defense, and Duke turned the ball over on downs. The Boilermakers had one more chance and nearly made good. With twenty-five seconds remaining, Gutman ran what appeared to be a routine QB sneak. However, after busting through the line, he turned and tossed a lateral to Jim Whitmer, who galloped 29 yards before getting out of bounds with seventeen seconds remaining. On the next play, Gutman dropped back and saw sophomore end Lamar Lundy break free in the Duke defensive backfield. The pass flew about a foot too high for the six-foot-seven Lundy on what would have surely been the winning score.

In the end, with the statistics nearly identical between the two sides, a tie was probably a just result, and the Boilermaker faithful went away feeling very good about their club.

September 29, 1956

Purdue 16, Missouri 7—"Jack the Ripper" Gets First Win

There were two significant debuts for the Boilermakers for the 1956 season opener against Missouri. At the pep rally before the game, "Purdue Pete" made his first physical appearance after more than a decade as a cartoon figure in University Bookstore advertisements. And on the sidelines, new head man Jack Mollenkopf led his team into battle.

The Boilermakers opened the game with an 85-yard scoring drive, capped off by a 3-yard scoring run by Mel Dillard. Len Dawson converted the PAT, and the home team led 7–0. That's how the score remained until early in the third quarter. Mizzou opened the second half with a 68-yard kick return to Purdue's 18. Two plays later, the game was tied at 7–7.

After the teams traded punts, halfback Tommy Fletcher made the play of the day for the Boilermakers. The junior halfback took a toss from Dawson around the left end. After changing directions twice, Fletcher picked up a few downfield blocks and broke into the open. Fletcher scampered 35 yards to pay dirt, leaving a trail of frustrated Missouri players on the ground behind

Above: By the mid-1950s, a completely transformed Ross-Ade stadium had a capacity of 55,500 and was ready for the greatest decade in program history. *Purdue Athletics.*

Left: Purdue Pete's debut on September 29, 1956, may have overshadowed the debut of rookie head coach Jack Mollenkopf, who go the first of his program-record eighty-four wins over Missouri. *Purdue Athletics.*

him. Late in the fourth quarter, with Missouri in the shadow of its own goal line, Lamar Lundy caused a Tiger fumble to trickle out the back of the end zone for the final two points of the day.

The Boilermakers ran for 304 yards on the day, while Dawson threw for another 118. It was a great offensive show and a sign of things to come for a program on the rise. The 16–7 margin gave Mollenkopf the first of his eighty-four wins at Purdue, a program record until Joe Tiller broke it four decades later. Even more enduring is the legacy of "Purdue Pete," who still stalks the sidelines at every Purdue game to this day.

October 27, 1956

No. 12 Iowa 21, Purdue 20—Heartbreak Against the Hawkeyes

The first month of the 1956 brought a little bit of everything for the Boilermakers. They opened with the hard-fought win over Missouri and then hit the road for three straight games: a tough loss at Minnesota, an upset win at no. 18 Notre Dame and a 6–6 tie against Wisconsin. The Boilers returned home to take on undefeated and 12th-ranked Iowa.

The Hawkeye offense did as it pleased in the first half, relying on misdirection and multiple handoffs to roll up 21 points in the first thirty minutes. Fortunately, the Purdue offense played nearly as well, scoring twice to trail by just 7 at the break. After a scoreless third quarter, Len Dawson hit Lamar Lundy for a 10-yard score with nine minutes to play in the game. Dawson pushed the PAT wide, and the Boilermakers trailed 21–20.

On Iowa's ensuing possession, defensive lineman John Jardine forced a fumble that the Boilers recovered near midfield. Mel Dillard ripped of a pair of runs to the Iowa 24 but fumbled; the home team seemed to be out of chances. The defense stiffened, however, and gave Dawson and company one more chance. An Iowa punt pinned Purdue back at the 4-yard line, 96 yards to go and less than three minutes to do so.

Dawson had done it before, leading his team on a 78-yard drive in the final minutes of the 1955 battle with the Hawkeyes in Iowa City, tossing the game-tying touchdown on the final play of the game. Here he had a chance to win it.

Dillard started off the drive with a 6-yard run to the 10. A 19-yard pass to Erich Barnes followed, but Iowa All-American lineman Alex

Quarterback Len Dawson looks to pitch to halfback John Brideweser, but the Boilermaker comeback falls just short against the eventual Rose Bowl champion Hawkeyes. *Purdue Athletics.*

Karras dropped Dawson for a 9-yard loss on the next snap. On second-and-19, Dawson called a screen pass to Dillard, who grabbed the pass and settled behind a wall of blockers. He was finally pushed out of bounds at the Hawkeye 35, a 45-yard gain to the home crowd's delight. Dawson connected with Bob Khoenle for 14, and the Boilermakers had a first down at the Iowa 21, 1:30 remaining.

The next play would be debated for years among those in attendance, as Dawson dropped back and swung a pass to the right flat to Barnes. Iowa linebacker Fred Harris hit Barnes just as the ball arrived and knocked it free. The officials ruled it a fumble, and the Hawkeyes recovered, ending the home team's final threat. After the game, Barnes was in disbelief. "I didn't have a chance," he said staring at the floor. "That guy hit me at the same time I got my hands on the ball and they call it a fumble."

Iowa went on to win the Big Ten and defeat Oregon State in the Rose Bowl, finishing no. 3 in the country. The Boilermakers finished 3-4-2 on the year, the only losing season in Mollenkopf's tenure.

October 18, 1958

Purdue 14, No. 5 Michigan State 6—Defensive Masterpiece Shuts Down Spartans

There was no way Purdue should have beaten Michigan State in 1958. The Spartans were defending national champions and focused on revenge. You see, MSU's one blemish in the 1957 title run was a 20–13 loss to Purdue. The Green and White came into the game undefeated and ranked fifth in the nation. Purdue had just gotten smacked around by Wisconsin, an ugly 31–6 loss in Madison.

What's more, Purdue lost five fumbles to the Spartans while turning the ball over six times total. It shouldn't have been a contest except for one thing: someone forgot to tell the Boilermaker defense.

In one of the greatest defensive performances in the history of Ross-Ade Stadium, Purdue held the vaunted Spartan ground attack to just 38 yards on forty-three carries. Through the air, MSU had just 58 yards and two interceptions. Michigan State came into the game averaging more than 190 yards rushing per game on the season. On this day, the Spartans would finish with just 96 yards of total offense, including a paltry 4 yards rushing in the second half.

The secret to Purdue's success was a throwback method implemented by Coach Jack Mollenkopf. The Boilermakers prepared two full units on defense and switched them in and out to keep fresh defenders on the field at all times. It allowed the home team to stay aggressive even as the visitors wore down.

Offensively, the Boilermakers did just enough with quarterback Ross Fichtner and fullback Bob Jarus leading the way on the ground. Jarus crashed in from the 1-yard line for the winning score, while Fichtner connected with Rich Brooks for the two-point conversion. Despite the six turnovers, Purdue gained 190 yards on the ground and 255 total offense on the day. It would suffice, thanks to one of the best defensive efforts in program history.

OCTOBER 3, 1959

PURDUE 28, No. 8 NOTRE DAME 7—FICHTNER FINISHES OFF IRISH

Legendary Purdue coach Jack Mollenkopf did a lot of things well while at the helm of the Boilermakers. Perhaps his most impressive accomplishment was his record against Notre Dame. Mollenkopf compiled a 9-4 record against the Irish, including seven wins while Notre Dame was ranked in the Top 10. That was the case when the golden-domers came to town in 1959.

More than fifty thousand fans packed into Ross-Ade Stadium and were delighted when the home team jumped out to an early lead. Senior quarterback Ross Fichtner led a ten-play scoring drive to start the game, with fullback Bob Jarus punching it in from 2 yards out to give the good guys the early lead. The Irish managed just one first down in the opening quarter, which came to a close with the Boilermakers once again driving.

Early in the second, Fichtner hit Rich Brooks for a 6-yard score, and the Boilermakers led 14–0. Notre Dame fumbled on the ensuing kickoff, and Purdue recovered. Seven plays later, Jarus was over the goal line for his second score of the day; in a game that was less than twenty minutes old,

Quarterback Ross Fichtner looks for Rich Brooks in the end zone to put Purdue up 14–0. Fichtner did enough to take down the Irish before a late injury sidelined him for the remainder of the 1959 season. *Purdue Athletics Film Archives.*

Purdue led 21–0. The Irish pieced together a touchdown drive early in the third quarter, but all hopes of a comeback were lost when Bernie Allen came up with a key interception for the Boilermakers late in the third.

The Purdue second team offense turned the good fortune into immediate points as junior halfback Jim Tiller took a handoff up the middle and saw the Notre Dame defense open up before his eyes. A quick dart to the right, and Tiller was off to the races, 74 yards to the end zone for the day's final score. It was the fourth time in six occasions the Boilermakers had beaten the Irish and, amazingly, the first time Purdue had ever won the Shillelagh Trophy in Ross-Ade Stadium.

The news wasn't all good for the home team, as late in the game, Fichtner would be lost for the season with a broken shoulder. He was the star for Purdue, rushing eleven times for 77 yards while leading the offensive and defensive backfields. Sadly, it would be his final game for the Boilermakers, but he went out a winner. Fichtner went on to play defensive back for nearly a decade for the Cleveland Browns and the New Orleans Saints.

OCTOBER 10, 1959

NO. 7 PURDUE 21, NO. 9 WISCONSIN 0—ANOTHER WEEK, ANOTHER TOP 10 WIN

Fresh off a dominant win over no. 8 Notre Dame, the Boilermakers got ready for another Top 10 opponent when no. 9 Wisconsin came to town. No team had the Boilermakers' number quite like the Badgers, with Wisconsin having posted a 9-0-1 record against Purdue in the previous ten meetings.

Junior quarterback Bernie Allen was thrust into the starting lineup with regular Ross Fichtner out for the year. It didn't take long for the replacement to make his mark. On Wisconsin's second play of the day, Allen intercepted a long Badger pass. He immediately led the home team on a 61-yard scoring drive that ended on a 12-yard pass to co-captain Len Jardine.

Allen would add two more scoring passes to complete the route, while the defense dominated the eventual Big Ten champion Badgers, allowing just 111 yards of total offense while forcing seven turnovers on the day. In the end, not even a torrential downpour, which lasted from the second quarter well into the postgame celebration, could dampen the spirits of the forty-one thousand Purdue fans in attendance.

Thrust into the lineup due to injury, quarterback Bernie Allen (no. 15) didn't miss a beat, starring in the win over Wisconsin. *Purdue Athletics Film Archive.*

The Boilermakers, with a second straight win over a Top 10 foe, would rise to no. 6 in the country when the next AP Poll was released. However, injuries sustained against Wisconsin led to a tough loss at Ohio State the following week. The Boilermakers finished the season 5-2-2 overall, 4-2-1 in the Big Ten, tied for second.

1960s

DECADE OF DOMINANCE

GRIESE, KEYES, PHIPPS AND THE ROSE BOWL

OCTOBER 15, 1960

PURDUE 24, NO. 3 OHIO STATE 21—WILLIE JONES DESTROYS
BUCKEYES' CHAMPIONSHIP HOPES

The 1960 campaign got off to an interesting start for Purdue with a season-opening tie against no. 8 UCLA, followed by a 51–19 destruction of no. 12 Notre Dame in South Bend in week two. The Boilermakers then fell on the road against unranked Wisconsin in week three, and as they prepared for third-ranked Ohio State in week four, no one was quite sure what Purdue was made of.

Meanwhile, Woody Hayes's team looked like an unstoppable force with shutout wins over USC and SMU to go along with a 34–7 demolishing of fourth-ranked Illinois. So, it was a shock to everyone when the Boilermakers ran up a 14–0 advantage early in the second quarter after two sustained drives ended in scoring plunges from fullback Willie Jones. They were the first two touchdowns for the senior from Robstown, Texas.

No one expected the Buckeyes to go quietly, and by halftime they had tied it up with a pair of touchdowns of their own. A Purdue drive to open the second half stalled, and Bernie Allen came in to kick a 38-yard field goal to put the home team up 17–14. The Buckeyes answered with a 74-yard scoring drive to take their first lead of the day, 21–17, late in the third quarter.

The Boilermakers answered right back, thanks in part to a personal foul against Ohio State. On first down from the Ohio State 26, Jones plunged through the middle of the line and then saw an opening to his left. Before the Buckeyes could react, Jones was standing in the end zone, with the day's final scoring run. He finished the day with 72 yards on just eleven carries and all three Purdue touchdowns. The home team had done what few had thought possible: toppled mighty Ohio State.

The Boilers would fall on the road to top-ranked Iowa the following week but took down no. 1 Minnesota late in the year, finishing with a pair of wins over top three foes for the first time in program history. It is a feat only matched by the 2021 Boilermakers, who took down no. 2 Iowa and no. 3 Michigan State in the same season.

OCTOBER 28, 1961

PURDUE 9, NO. 5 IOWA 0—HOMECOMING SHUTOUT

Acting head coach Bob DeMoss saw it coming. He told his team so at the beginning of the week. The Iowa Hawkeyes hadn't been shut out in nearly a decade, a span of 78 games. But "DeMo" knew that his squad had the means to hold the Hawks off the scoreboard. It had been a rough few weeks for the Boilermakers. After starting the season 2-1 with wins over Washington and Miami (OH) and a 22–20 setback against Notre Dame, the Boilermakers dropped a heartbreaker in Ann Arbor when a first-quarter fumble out of the end zone proved to be the difference in a 16–14 loss to Michigan.

But worse than any loss suffered on the field was the fact that Head Coach Jack Mollenkopf was forced to leave the team on the eve of the Big Ten season for surgery to have a tumor removed from his lower abdomen. It was hoped that he would return in a few weeks, but that was unknown. It was certain that he wouldn't be back by the time no. 5 Iowa came to town.

The Hawkeyes actually began the year ranked no. 1 in the AP Poll but had fallen to 5th despite a perfect 4-0 record. But there were weaknesses in this squad, and DeMoss thought that his Boilers could exploit them. Purdue got an assist from Mother Nature, as game day dawned with pouring rain. Iowa received the opening kickoff and almost immediately turned it over, with defensive lineman Don Paltani grabbing an interception. On the ensuing possession, quarterback Ron DiGravio converted two fourth-and-1 situations with sneaks before plunging through the middle of the line for the day's first points. A bad snap led to a failed PAT attempt, and the home team led 6–0.

The Boilermakers emerged from the halftime locker room in a fresh set of uniforms, much to the delight of the Homecoming crowd. At least for a little while, they could read the numbers of their squad again rather than seeing eleven mud-soaked men running around anonymously. The driving rain continued throughout the game, and the mud was ankle deep on the field. Purdue delighted the home crowd further with a third-quarter field goal to extend the lead to 9–0. Meanwhile, Purdue's defensive effort on the day was among the best in program history. Iowa turned the ball over five times and gained just 185 yards of total offense, more than 200 yards less than their average on the year.

Mollenkopf returned to West Lafayette the following Tuesday and resumed his duties in time for the road trip to Illinois, but not before DeMoss was named the UPI's National Coach of the Week for his efforts against Iowa.

November 11, 1961

Purdue 7, No. 6 Michigan State 6—Brumm for the Block

Fresh off a 23–9 win at Illinois, the Boilermakers had a chance to test themselves against another one of the nation's best when no. 6 Michigan State came to town. The Spartans had spent the entire season in the Top 10 and three weeks at the top spot of the AP Poll. Legendary head coach Duffy Daugherty was in his eighth season and was on phenomenal run of success for the Green and White.

Jack Mollenkopf, meanwhile, was just happy to be back roaming the sidelines for Purdue, with his emergency surgery less than a month in the rear-view mirror. It would once again be the Boilermaker defense that led the team to victory.

Michigan State got on the board early in the second quarter on an 11-yard run by fullback George Saimes. But a great play by Purdue tackle Don Brumm on the PAT would prove to be vital. Brumm busted through the line on the point after and got a hand up to deflect the kick. MSU's lead remained 6–0. Late in the half, Purdue drove 61 yards down to the Michigan State 1. But the defense held, and the visitors carried their lead into the break.

Midway through the third quarter, the Boilermakers once again put together a 61-yard drive. But this one went the distance, as Ron DiGravio hit halfback Tom Boris for a 15-yard score to tie the game with the PAT still to go. Junior kicker Skip Ohl split the uprights on what would end up being the final point of the afternoon.

It was another defensive masterpiece by the Boilermakers, as they held MSU to just 195 yards of total offense, well below their season average of 330 yards per game. Michigan State would win its final two games to finish the season no. 8 in the AP Poll. The Boilermakers hit the road for a Top 10 matchup with no. 5 Minnesota the following week and came up just short of their third major upset of the season, falling 10–7. However, Mollenkopf kept his perfect record in the Old Oaken Bucket game intact, closing the season with a 34–12 win over Indiana to finish 6-3 overall in what was an exciting, if tumultuous, season.

NOVEMBER 21, 1964

PURDUE 28, INDIANA 22—TETER THRILLS RECORD CROWD

Conditions were brutal for the final game of the 1964 season, with the temperature at kickoff settling at fifteen degrees with a stiff wind out of the north making it feel worse. Snow covered the bleachers of Ross-Ade Stadium after several inches had fallen late in the week. But none of these facts deterred the record crowd of more than 61,700 people from turning out.

What they witnessed was a heroic effort by junior halfback Gordon Teter and a dominant victory for the home team, despite the final score. Indiana actually got on the board early for a 7–0 lead. After Teter tied it up with a 2-yard scoring run, the Hoosiers again scored to go up 14–7 early in the second quarter. Sophomore quarterback Bob Griese connected with Rich Ruble for a 25-yard scoring toss, and the game was knotted at 14–14 at the half.

The Boilermakers opened the third quarter with a dominant drive, going 74 yards on sixteen plays, all on the ground. When Teter crashed over the goal line for his second score of the day, more than eight minutes had come off the clock and the home team had taken the lead for good. After IU missed a field goal, the Boilermakers went on another sustained drive to put the game out of reach. This time, Griese engineered an 80-yard drive on seventeen plays, and by the time Randy Minniear hit pay dirt, less than

Head Coach Jack Mollenkopf gives Gordon Teter a hug following a heroic effort against Indiana, rushing for 126 yards and two scores. *Purdue Athletics.*

six minutes remained in the contest. IU scored eight points in the closing seconds to make the final score appear closer than the game itself was.

Teter finished with 126 yards on thirty-one carries, both totals surpassing the entire Hoosier rushing effort on the day. At the annual Kiwanis Club banquet two days later, senior defensive end Harold Wells assisted "Pop" Doan in adding yet another "P" to the Old Oaken Bucket. It was the fifteenth time in the last seventeen years that Purdue had claimed the Bucket in the most dominant stretch in the history of the series.

September 25, 1965

No. 6 Purdue 25, No. 1 Notre Dame 21—Griese Nearly Perfect Over Irish

During his sophomore season, quarterback Bob Griese showed flashes of his potential. He threw for nearly 1,000 yards and five scores while earning the team's Outstanding Sophomore honor. But it was during the second game of the 1965 season that he truly arrived.

Left: Quarterback Bob Griese had to be perfect to take down no. 1 Notre Dame in 1965. He was, completing nineteen of twenty-two for 283 yards and three scores while also rushing for 39 yards. *Purdue Athletics.*

Below: The final scoreboard told the tale: the Boilermakers had vanquished no. 1 Notre Dame. *Purdue Athletics Film Archive.*

Victorious over Miami (Ohio) in the season opener, the Boilermakers welcomed top-ranked Notre Dame to Ross-Ade Stadium in week two. The Irish had destroyed California to open the season, and everyone knew that it would take something special to compete with them. What Griese delivered was near perfection.

Nearly sixty-two thousand fans packed into Ross-Ade to see no. 6 Purdue take on the top-ranked Irish on a sun-splashed afternoon. Notre Dame got on the board late in the first quarter with a short field goal. The Boilermakers responded with a 74-yard scoring drive, with Griese hitting sophomore end Jim Beirne for a 28-yard score. Griese missed the PAT, and the score stayed 6–3. The Irish went on top 10–6 on a Nick Eddy touchdown, but Griese and Beirne connected again for a 14-yard score and a 12–10 lead just before halftime, with the star receiver making a spectacular diving catch in the end zone.

Randy Minniear put the home team up 18–10 after catching a Griese pass and rumbling 12 yards to pay dirt. But a second two-point conversion failed. The Fighting Irish scored late in the third quarter and converted their two-point try, so the final stanza began with the score knotted at 18–18.

The teams opened the fourth quarter by trading punts before Notre Dame put together a drive. The Irish had first-and-goal from the 7 before the Purdue defense stiffened, forcing a field goal try. The 24-yard kick by Ken Ivan bounced off the crossbar and through to give the Irish a 21–18 lead. The problem was that they left Griese more than five minutes to work his magic.

The Boilermakers took over at their 33-yard line. On first down, Griese hit flanker Jim Finley for 32 yards down the sideline. Just like that, Purdue was inside Notre Dame territory. Wasting no time pressing his advantage, Griese hit Beirne for 13 yards across the middle and then went back to the sophomore for 19 more yards down to the Notre Dame 3. Purdue had gained 70 yards on three plays, to the delight of the home crowd. The next snap was a more conservative call, but it was no less successful; left tackle Karl Singer and left guard Sal Ciampi tore a hole in the defensive line, and Gordon Teter crossed the goal line untouched, giving the good guys the 25–21 win.

On the day, Griese was 19 of 22 through the air for 283 yards and three scores. He also ran for 39 yards on the day and set single-game records for completions, completion percentage, passing yards and total offense. His legend was only just beginning.

November 19, 1966

No. 10 Purdue 51, Indiana 6—Senior Day Spectacular Has Griese Smelling Roses

The 1966 season was one for the ages for Purdue. Their only two losses were on the road against the top two teams in America. And they had laid waste to the rest of the schedule, averaging more than 28 points in each win while shutting out three conference opponents for the first time in more than three decades.

As they prepared for the Old Oaken Bucket showdown with Indiana, a trip to the Rose Bowl was already ensured after beating Minnesota the previous week. The rivalry matchup would be all about bragging rights and sending off a great senior class the right way, chief among them quarterback Bob Griese.

The record crowd of 62,197 fans got their money's worth. On their second possession of the game, Griese dropped back and hit halfback Jim Finley, who was split wide right. The senior from Streator, Illinois, made two Hoosiers miss and then took off across the field, where he picked up a wall of blockers; 80 yards later, the Boilermakers were on the board. The floodgates really opened in the second quarter, with Griese scoring on a quarterback sneak and sophomore Leroy Keyes scoring on a 7-yard run to go up 21–0.

The offense got the ball back with three minutes to go in the half. Griese connected with halfback Bob Baltzell for a 67-yard score. Three plays later, Keyes intercepted a pass, and the Boilermaker offense was back in business. Keyes took a toss from Griese and hit receiver Jim Beirne for a 12-yard scoring pass. Indiana fumbled the kickoff, and Chuck Kyle jumped on it, giving the Boilermakers yet another scoring opportunity. Short on time, Griese missed a field goal attempt, but Indiana was penalized for being offside. Given another shot to score, Griese dropped back and hit Beirne for another touchdown. At the half, the home team led 41–0, having scored three times in the final three minutes.

Griese added a field goal and a second rushing touchdown in the third quarter to make it 51–0 for the good guys. On the day, Griese threw for three scores, ran for two more and added six PATs to his 24-yard field goal. He finished with 255 passing yards in his final Ross-Ade appearance. He owned virtually every passing and scoring record in program history, finished as the runner-up for the 1966 Heisman Trophy and, of course, won his final game for Purdue when the Boilermakers defeated USC 14–13 in Pasadena.

Quarterback Bob Griese and halfback Leroy Keyes caused many a nightmare for opposing defenses in their short time together, leading the Boilermakers to the Rose Bowl. *Purdue Athletics*.

SEPTEMBER 30, 1967

NO. 10 PURDUE 28, NO. 1 NOTRE DAME 21—TOO MANY HEROES TO LIST

Week two of the 1967 season set up to be an epic showdown. Purdue had opened the year with an impressive win over Texas A&M at the Cotton Bowl. The Boilermakers would welcome a top-ranked Notre Dame team that had handled Cal in week one in South Bend. The Irish were defending national champs and heavily favored to repeat in 1967. Their backfield featured All-American quarterback Terry Hanratty and fullback Rocky Bleier, who would go on to win four Super Bowls in Pittsburgh.

On the other side, sophomore quarterback Mike Phipps was making just his second career start in his bid to replace the irreplaceable Bob Griese. Purdue received the opening kick and drove right down field, with Phipps connecting with Jim Beirne for a 40-yard gain and fullback Perry Williams scoring from 10 yards out. Bob Baltzell missed the PAT, and Purdue led 6–0. The Irish scored near the end of the opening quarter on a Hanratty sneak and carried their 7–6 lead into the half.

On their first drive of the second half, Phipps came up with a huge fourth-down conversion, hitting Baltzell for a 34-yard gain. Williams again found the end zone, and Phipps and Beirne connected for a two-point conversion to make it 14–7. Bleier scored near the end of the third quarter to make it 14–14 with fifteen minutes to play.

On their next possession, the Boilermakers drove 64 yards, with Leroy Keyes doing most of the work, first on a leaping 44-yard reception down the sideline and then with an 11-yard touchdown catch. The lead barely lasted two minutes as Hanratty hit Paul Snow for a 27-yard score to pull the Irish even once more. On the ensuing drive, Phipps converted a third-and-long by finding Baltzell streaking down the seam from his halfback position. After making the catch and a slick cut across the field that caused two Irish defenders to run into each other, Baltzell waltzed into the end zone to put the home team up for good, 28–21.

The Irish had a few chances to tie the game, but linebacker Dick Marvel made his twentieth tackle of the day on a key fourth-down stop in the red zone and Leroy Keyes intercepted a desperation throw from Hanratty in the final minutes. On the day, the Irish won the statistical battle, outgaining Purdue by more than 130 yards. Hanratty attempted a school-record sixty-three passes on the day, nearly double the attempts Phipps made on the day. But he also threw four interceptions as the Boilermaker secondary took advantage of the Irish aggression.

Purdue would go on to win a share of the Big Ten title while climbing as high as no. 2 in the nation, finishing the year at 8-2. But the same rule that allowed them to go to the Rose Bowl after the 1966 season left them home following the 1967 season.

OCTOBER 19, 1968

NO. 5 PURDUE 28, WAKE FOREST 27—LEROY GIVETH, LEROY (NEARLY) TAKETH AWAY

The beginning of the 1968 season could not have gone better for the Boilermakers. Ranked no. 1 in the nation when the season began, the Boilermakers dominated Virginia in the opener and then took care of no. 2 Notre Dame in South Bend and beat up on Northwestern. The season hit a speed bump when the top-ranked Boilermakers lost at no. 4 Ohio State. As the Boilermakers returned home to take on Wake Forest, the margin for error was razor thin if the team wanted to achieve its goals.

Unfortunately for the Boilermakers, the errors against the Demon Deacons were plentiful. The visitors took an early lead with a field goal after Leroy Keyes fumbled on Purdue's second play and then extended it with a touchdown early in the second quarter following another Keyes fumble. Fullback Perry Williams finally got Purdue on the board, but the Deacons had the final word in the first half and led 17–7 at the break before nearly fifty-eight thousand stunned Boilermaker faithful. The score was bad enough, but the real shocker was that Purdue's star running back had gifted 10 points to the opposition with a pair of fumbles.

Keyes atoned for his first-half sins with a brilliant 19-yard touchdown run in the third quarter as he took a pitch to the left, cut to hit an alley between two defenders and then made five more miss him on the way to pay dirt. Wake's next possession went nowhere, but a great punt pinned Purdue deep. On a third-down run play, Keyes again coughed it up, and the Deacons took over at the Purdue 7-yard line. Three plays later, their lead was back to 10. They added a field goal early in the fourth quarter, and with less than twelve minutes remaining, the Boilermakers trailed 27–14.

Another promising Purdue drive ended with Keyes's fourth fumble of the afternoon, and it appeared that this one might be the back-breaker. Wake could not capitalize and had to punt. However, the Boilermakers were down by two scores, and just seven minutes remained. Keyes caught a pass for 26 yards to keep the drive alive. On the next play, with Leroy's number being called again, he actually decided to switch places with backfield mate Jim Kirkpatrick because of a sore knee. Kirkpatrick rumbled 14 yards for the score, and the Boilermakers were within one score, 27–21.

The defense was able to get the ball back, but the Purdue offense would be severely hampered as quarterback Mike Phipps was done for the day with an ankle injury and Keyes was banged up, nursing knee, wrist and back injuries. Backup QB Don Kiepert quickly faced a fourth-and-8 situation. He dropped back to pass and was flushed from the pocket. Then he saw open field in front of him. Kiepert scrambled for 11 yards to keep the drive alive. Six plays later, Keyes carried the ball across the goal line, and the comeback was complete.

Leroy had a day to remember. He ran for 214 yards and two scores, including the game winner in the closing minutes. He also fumbled six times, lost four of them and saw the opponent convert them into seventeen points.

NOVEMBER 23, 1968

No. 12 PURDUE 38, INDIANA 35—THE GREATEST SENIOR DAY EVER

Senior Day 1968 was a celebration of maybe the most accomplished group in Purdue history. As sophomores, they had won the Rose Bowl. They followed that up with a Big Ten title as juniors and spent a third of their senior season ranked no. 1 in the nation. Now there was just one thing left to do: beat Indiana and get back the Old Oaken Bucket. The Hoosiers had won the 1967 contest to clinch a share of the Big Ten title and a trip to the Rose Bowl. It was just their second win in the series in twenty years, and as far as the Boilermakers were concerned, that was plenty.

The team had the added motivation of closing out the season on the right note for their head coach. In late October, Jack Mollenkopf took ill and was rushed to the hospital, diagnosed with hepatitis. Now four weeks later, the coach was still in the hospital, and top assistant Bob DeMoss was temporarily at the helm once more.

In an emotional scene in the Purdue locker room just before kickoff, Mollenkopf surprised everyone with a visit. His pregame speech to the team

For two solid years, this shout rang out across Ross-Ade Stadium: "Give the ball to Leroy!" It was sound advice. *Purdue Athletics.*

left many of the men in tears and some struggling to stay focused on the job at hand. It showed.

Indiana forced a Purdue punt, and on their second offensive play, Bob Pernell burst through the line and went 64 yards for a score. Leroy Keyes evened things up with a 41-yard scoring run halfway through the quarter, but IU took the lead back late in the first. Purdue added a field goal early in the second quarter, but the Hoosiers struck late, finding the end zone with a minute remaining in the half. The visitors led 21–10 at the break. They extended that lead to 28–10 before Perry Williams got the Boilermakers back on the board with a 2-yard run.

The teams traded punts, and as the fourth quarter began, the Boilermakers had the ball, down eleven. Mike Phipps completed three straight passes, with Bob Dillingham snaring two of them, moving the ball to the 3-yard line. Keyes crashed over the goal line for his second score, and the Boilers were within four.

Indiana extended the lead back to eleven on a long touchdown pass, and things began to look dire for Purdue. They needed two scores, and less than ten minutes remained in their season. Luckily, DeMoss listened to the battle cry from Purdue fans, who had spent the last two years screaming, "Give the ball to Leroy!"

Phipps dropped back to pass and rolled to his right to avoid the rush. At first, the quarterback looked like he might take off and run. He then saw the impossible: Keyes had found his way behind every Indiana defender. Phipps put every ounce of energy into the throw, and 60 yards later, Keyes settled under it at the goal line. Indiana's lead was cut to 35–31.

The defense finally forced a punt, and Leroy and company would have one more chance. Phipps started the drive connecting on his first four passes for 45 yards. After running for a first down, Phipps hit Greg Fenner for 26 yards down to the 1-yard line. On the next play, Leroy followed Perry Williams up the middle for the go-ahead score. The Boilermakers took the lead for the first time all game. The defense forced a turnover on downs, allowing Keyes, Williams and Dillingham to each get curtain calls, coming off the field to standing ovations from the record crowd.

In his final game, Leroy was spectacular. He ended with 140 rushing yards, 149 receiving yards and four total touchdowns. Even more impressive was classmate Chuck Kyle, who recorded twenty-seven total tackles on the day, a record that still stands today. Both men would be named consensus All-Americans after the season.

SEPTEMBER 27, 1969

NO. 16 PURDUE 28, NO. 9 NOTRE DAME 14—THREE-PEAT FOR PHIPPS

At the dawn of the 1969 season, few teams in college football history had beaten Notre Dame three consecutive years, and no starting quarterbacks had ever vanquished the Irish three times. That's what was on the line for Mike Phipps and the Boilermakers when Notre Dame came to Ross-Ade in week two of the season.

As a sophomore, Phipps led Purdue to an upset of the top-ranked Irish. As a junior, he led the no. 1 Boilermakers to a double-digit win over no. 2 Notre Dame in South Bend. Now he would have one more shot at the premier program in college football history.

Phipps got the Boilers on the board late in the first quarter with a 37-yard scoring pass to Randy Cooper. Stan Brown added a 2-yard touchdown run in the second quarter, and the home team led 14–0. Irish quarterback Joe Thiesmann got half of it back with a touchdown pass just before the break, and Purdue had to settle for a 14–7 lead at the half.

The Boilermakers scored on back-to-back possessions in the second half, a 1-yard sneak by Phipps and a 2-yard run by Brown, and led 28–7 early in the fourth. Theismann threw a second touchdown pass late for the final tally of the day.

Phipps finished 12 of 20 for 213 yards and a score through the air to go with his rushing touchdown. He was one of seven seniors who played in all three games and could forever say that they never lost to the Irish. Unbeknownst to anyone at the time, it would also be the final time Head Coach Jack Mollenkopf would face Notre Dame as well. His sudden retirement after the season brought to a close one of the most successful runs any coach in history had against the Notre Dame, as he finished with a 10-4 record in the series.

OCTOBER 4, 1969

NO. 8 PURDUE 36, NO. 17 STANFORD 35—PHIPPS VS. PLUNKETT

Fresh off a victorious dual against future College Football Hall of Famer Joe Theismann, quarterback Mike Phipps got ready to dual with another burgeoning legend when Jim Plunkett brought his Stanford squad to town. Plunkett, who would go on to win the Heisman Trophy in 1971 and be selected first overall by the New England Patriots, was just a sophomore for Stanford, but he was already being recognized as one of the nation's best.

More than sixty-five thousand people packed into Ross-Ade on a sun-splashed early October afternoon to see this showdown. What they witnessed far exceeded the expectations of anyone in attendance.

The two teams traded blows throughout the first half, with Phipps throwing for three scores and Plunkett tossing two touchdowns. But it was even at the break, 21–21.

Stanford dominated the third quarter, with Plunkett throwing two more scores to take a 35–21 lead into the fourth. The teams traded punts to start the final frame, and then Phipps went to work, covering 80 yards on just three plays and hitting John Bullock for the final 21 yards to make it 35–28. Plunkett drove Stanford to the Purdue 7-yard line, but the drive stalled and the visitors missed on a 25-yard field goal that would've pushed the lead back to 10. The Boilers had life once more.

After seeing a drive stall thanks to untimely penalties, the Boilermakers turned it over on downs and would once again need the defense to save the day. The unit that had given up 35 points on the day finally stiffened, forcing a three-and-out and a Stanford punt. Phipps would have one more chance with four minutes to go, 79 yards from the goal line.

On first down, Phipps dropped back and found a streaking Randy Cooper on the right sideline. Cooper was completely ignored by the defense coming out of the backfield, and he was at top speed as Phipps hit him in stride. When the defense finally pushed him out of bounds 65 yards later, the roar of the crowd was deafening. On the next snap, Phipps began to scramble to his left. The mobile quarterback then relied on a move that he had perfected in three seasons for the Boilermakers, feinting a run only to level out at the last second and fire a pass downfield. It worked to perfection as the defense began to cheat toward the line, leaving Stan Brown all alone in the end zone. Two plays, 79 yards and a score made it 35–34 Stanford and left Coach Mollenkopf with a decision to make.

Sensing that the momentum was all on their side, the Boilermakers went for two points and the win. Phipps took the snap and began rolling right. As the defense tracked him toward the sideline, the senior signal caller planted and threw back toward the middle of the field, where end Greg Fenner cradled the ball and fell to the ground, giving Purdue the 36–35 lead. Defensive back Mike Renie dashed Stanford's last hope, intercepting Plunkett's final pass on the day.

Plunkett was great, throwing for 355 yards and four scores. But Mike Phipps was in a class by himself, completing 28 of 39 for 429 yards and five scores, all of which set single-game records for the Boilermakers. His passing yardage was 138 yards more than his own previous record versus Indiana in 1968. And in the final two scoring drives, when his team needed him the most, Phipps went five for five for 159 yards and two scores while also converting the two-point try. It was maybe the greatest command performance in Ross-Ade Stadium history.

November 8, 1969

No. 10 Purdue 41, Michigan State 13—Mollenkopf's Swan Song

Senior Day 1969 was devoid of much of the drama that is a feature of many games on this list. The Boilermakers made quick work of Michigan State in a 41–13 final. Purdue's offense had finished scoring before the Spartans got on the board with two fourth-quarter touchdowns. Senior quarterback Mike Phipps threw for 292 yards and moved into seventh-place on the NCAA list for career passing yards. Stan Brown was the star of the day, with seven receptions for 152 yards to go along with a pair of rushing touchdowns.

But while the game may have not been a thriller, it was certainly significant for reasons no one knew at the time. It was the final Ross-Ade triumph for the great Jack Mollenkopf. A little more than a month after the 1969 season was over, Mollenkopf announced his retirement, citing a desire to take life easy after what had been a stressful professional life. He was sixty-five years old and had a few health scares over the years, including two that forced him

Jack Mollenkopf retired following the 1969 season, which also saw the graduation of All-Americans Mike Phipps (*left*) and Tim Foley (*right*). *Purdue Athletics.*

to miss multiple games. He was healthy again following the 1969 season and elected to enjoy life a bit more instead of asking the board of trustees for an exemption on the university's mandatory retirement.

Mollenkopf came to Purdue as an assistant to Stu Holcomb in time for the 1947 season. Nine years later, after taking over the program when Holcomb left to become the athletics director at Northwestern, Jack led Purdue to a level of success never before seen in West Lafayette. The Boilermakers had one losing season in Mollenkopf's fourteen years at the helm, finishing in the top three in the Big Ten on seven occasions. Purdue finished 8-2 or better in each of his final four seasons, including winning the 1967 Rose Bowl and a share of the 1967 Big Ten title. He coached fourteen All-Americans and three men who finished as runners up for the Heisman Trophy.

This victory over Michigan State put a bow on Mollenkopf's Ross-Ade record of 47-12-3, which included winning thirty of his last thirty-three games at home. Two weeks later, the Boilermakers concluded the 1969 season with a 44–21 win at Indiana. It was Mollenkopf's 86th and final win at Purdue. Fitting that it came against the in-state rival that he had owned over the years. Mollenkopf's teams dominated all three trophy rivalries with stellar records against Illinois (8-4-2), Notre Dame (10-4) and Indiana (11-2-1).

1970s
TRANSITIONS

ARMSTRONG, YOUNG AND HERRMANN

November 25, 1972

Purdue 41, Indiana 7—Otis Goes Off

Heading into the final game of his Purdue career, running back Otis Armstrong was having a fine senior season. He already had set the single-season rushing record for the Boilermakers and became the career rushing leader as well. He set the single-game rushing record earlier in the season with 233 yards in a 37–0 Homecoming romp over Northwestern. And, as it turned out, he was saving the best for last.

Just a year prior in Bloomington, the Old Oaken Bucket contest was marred by a bench-clearing brawl after Purdue quarterback Gary Danielson was hit late out of bounds and then kicked in the face. While the 1972 Bucket game lacked that type of drama, Otis made up for it.

Armstrong got the ball early and often, scoring on a 2-yard run in the first quarter. Danielson hooked up with Darryl Stingley for a 79-yard touchdown in the second quarter, and the Boilers led 14–7 at the half. Two plays into the second half, Otis took a handoff up the middle on a play designed to gain a few yards. Barely keeping his balance on the cold, soggy turf, Armstrong sprinted through the defense and found himself all alone in the end zone 71 yards later, giving his squad a 21–7 lead.

He added a 53-yard scoring run in the fourth quarter, and when the final gun sounded, the home team was victorious, 42–7. Armstrong was spectacular, breaking his single-game record with 276 rushing yards to go with three scores. He closed out his career as the Big Ten's all-time leading rusher, his three-year total of 3,315 yards breaking the four-year record of 1954 Heisman Trophy winner Alan Ameche. Armstrong was named Big Ten Player of the Year and was a first-round selection for the Denver Broncos. And he almost single-handedly made sure that the Senior Day for himself, Danielson, Stingley, Dave Butz and Gregg Bingham was a rousing success.

November 15, 1975

Purdue 19, Iowa 18—The Five-Minute Miracle

The Boilermakers have dominated few opponents over the years more than the Iowa Hawkeyes during the 1960s and 1970s. Beginning with the shutout win over no. 5 Iowa in 1961, Purdue had won fourteen straight in the series when Iowa came to town late in 1975, and this contest appeared to be more of the same from the opening kick. Purdue went on a nineteen-play, 86-yard scoring drive, with Scott Dierking covering the final 2 yards for the touchdown. What's more, the Boilermakers exerted their dominance by running the ball on all nineteen snaps, using up nearly the entire first quarter.

However, the Hawkeyes scored the next 18 points and were in control with less than ten minutes to go. The winning streak seemingly over, many of the 45,500 fans in attendance began heading for the exits, not wanting to see their team fall to 2-8 on the year. Instead, they missed a heroic effort by several Boilermakers.

Quarterback Mark Vitali led a ten-play, 69-yard scoring drive, with Dierking scoring from 4 yards out to cut the lead to 18–13 with 5:15 left on the clock. The defense forced a punt, and the home team got the ball back with three and a half minutes remaining, down by five.

After a first-down run to midfield by fullback Mike Pruitt, three plays went nowhere for the Boilermakers as they faced a fourth-and-10 situation. To make matters worse, Vitali was injured on the previous play, and backup QB Craig Nagel had to come in off the bench for the biggest play of the game. Nagel took the snap and dropped back, firing a strike to receiver Reggie Arnold, who made a leaping grab for 23 yards and a first down. Nagel's next three passes fell incomplete, and he once again faced a fourth-

Scott Dierking goes over the top for the winning score against Iowa, with five seconds to spare. *Purdue Athletics.*

and-long situation. This time, he found flanker Paul Beery, who made a diving catch at the 8-yard line for another first down.

On first-and-goal, Dierking took a pitch to the left and gained 5 yards. The same play on second down gained 2 more yards, and with twenty-seven seconds remaining, the Boilermakers were a yard from the goal line. Head Coach Alex Agase took his final timeout and called two plays, in case the first one failed to gain the required yard. As it happened, both play calls were the same: Dierking diving over the middle of the line.

On third down, Dierking took the handoff and leaped toward the end zone. He was ruled short, and the offense scrambled to get set for one final attempt. This time he found the promised land. Iowa head coach Bob Commings sprinted onto the field, adamant that Dierking was short of the goal line, but the call stood as the home side snatched victory from the jaws of defeat with five seconds to spare.

NOVEMBER 6, 1976

PURDUE 16, NO. 1 MICHIGAN 14—TOPPLING A GIANT

On September 30, 1972, the Michigan football team entered the Associate Press Top 10, checking in at no. 8 after taking down 6th-ranked UCLA. Over the course of the next seven seasons, they would spend exactly one week outside the Top 10. That was the level of excellence the Wolverines brought to Ross-Ade Stadium in early November 1976. What's more, the '76 version of the Wolverines had been a juggernaut from the start, outscoring opponents by an average of 44–7, shutting out half of the teams they'd faced so far and never scoring fewer than 31 points in a game.

Purdue, meanwhile, was in the midst of a middling season, a three-game losing streak bringing the season ledger to 3-5 overall. Head Coach Alex Agase was in his fourth season at the helm, and a fifth year was looking less likely every week.

The game started about as poorly as possible for the Boilermakers. A first-quarter fumble led to a quick Michigan lead, with quarterback Rick Leach scoring from 8 yards out. The Purdue offense responded with a score of its own, with Scott Dierking tying the game up late in the first quarter. Dierking added a 25-yard scoring jaunt in the second quarter, although a blocked PAT left the score 13–7 at the half.

The Wolverines opened the second half with a statement drive, with big gains taking the ball deep into Purdue territory. That is when the tide began to turn. With a first-and-goal from the 4-yard line, the Purdue defense transformed into a brick wall. The first three plays yielded just 3 yards, and on fourth-and-goal from the 1, a fumbled pitch led to a 15-yard loss and a turnover on downs. Michigan would eventually take the lead on a 64-yard touchdown pass from Leach to Jim Smith, but the belief created on that goal-line stand was undeniable.

Early in the fourth quarter, the Wolverines were driving, looking to extend their lead, when another fumble killed the drive. The Boilermakers then went on a fifteen-play drive, calling a dozen run plays and taking several minutes off the clock. When sophomore kicker Rock Suppan booted home a 23-yard field goal with just over four minutes remaining, the Boilermakers took the lead for good, 16–14. Mighty Michigan had fallen.

The Purdue offense hung with the top team in the country largely by controlling the ball. The Boilermakers ran fifteen more plays than Michigan, and Scott Dierking had a school-record thirty-eight carries on the day for 162 yards, plus a pair of touchdowns, outperforming Michigan's All-American running back Rob Lytle.

September 24, 1977

No. 11 Notre Dame 31, Purdue 24—Waking a Legend

The 1977 Battle for the Shillelagh couldn't have started much better for the Boilermakers. Purdue opened the game with a field goal, and then freshman quarterback Mark Herrmann hit Reggie Arnold for a touchdown; the home team led 10–0 after one. The Irish took a lead in the second quarter on a pair of touchdown throws from Rusty Lisch to Terry Eurick, but Purdue kept pace. Herrmann hit Ray Smith on a 37-yard touchdown and then connected with Russell Pope for a 43-yard score to put the home team back up 24–14 at the half.

To make matters worse for the Irish, they were playing musical quarterbacks. Lisch had started the game, but Coach Dan Devine pulled him in the first quarter, inserting backup Gary Forystek. Lisch had to come back into the game in the second quarter when Purdue linebacker Fred Arrington knocked Forystek out of the game.

After a scoreless third quarter, the Boilermakers brought out Scott Sovereen for a field goal attempt. The kick was good, but the home team was guilty of illegal procedure and 3 points came off the board. Sovereen missed from 5 yards farther back, and the score remained 24–14.

Devine had seen enough of Lisch and decided to bring his third-string quarterback in, senior Joe Montana. Montana hadn't played as a freshman, per university rules. He split time as a sophomore in 1975 and then missed the entire 1976 season due to injury. By the beginning of 1977, he was buried on the depth chart under a head coach who hadn't recruited him.

Montana led the Irish into scoring position with three completions for 70 yards, and the visiting team kicked a short field goal to pull within a touchdown, 24–17. Herrmann threw an interception on Purdue's next drive, and Montana drove a short field, hitting tight end Ken MacAfee for a touchdown to tie the game with ten minutes remaining.

The teams traded punts before Notre Dame once again took over near midfield. Three straight completions for Montana brought the ball inside the 10-yard line with two minutes to go. Two plays later, Mitchell crashed into the end zone for the day's final score. It was the first time all afternoon that the Boilermakers had trailed.

In less than a quarter, Montana went 9 for 14 for 154 yards and a score, leading the improbable comeback from the third string. He would start the rest of the season for the Irish, as they finished the year 11-1, demolished top-ranked Texas in the Cotton Bowl and won the national title.

OCTOBER 14, 1978

PURDUE 27, NO. 16 OHIO STATE 16—YOUNG, HERRMANN BREAK THROUGH

Jim Young's first season at Purdue showed signs of things to come, but when the 1977 campaign was over, the team's record was the same as his predecessor's: 5-6 after a loss to Indiana in the final week. Year two was off to a much better start with a 3-1 record in the first month, but it wasn't until week five that Young and the Boilermakers truly announced their arrival to the college football world.

Woody Hayes brought no. 16 Ohio State to town with a 2-1-1 record, but they were still among the favorites to win the Big Ten. The game got off to a slow start with the Boilermakers getting a first-quarter field goal and the Buckeyes answering with a second-quarter touchdown, for a 7–3 game at the half. On the opening drive of the second half, sophomore quarterback Mark Herrmann completed 7 of 10 pass attempts before halfback John Macon scored from a yard out.

After the Buckeyes tied the game at 10–10, Russ Pope scored from 11 yards out to put the home team back on top, 17–10. Kicker Scott Sovereen booted the nineteenth field goal of his career early in the fourth quarter to extend the lead to 10 and take over the top spot in program history. The Buckeyes pulled within 4, but when Herrmann connected with flanker Mike Harris from 19 yards out for his only scoring pass of the day, it was the final nail in the coffin.

Thanks to Michigan State upsetting no. 5 Michigan, the Boilermakers ended the afternoon alone atop the Big Ten standings. A tie at Wisconsin cost the Boilermakers a share of the Big Ten title, but they did earn an invitation to the Peach Bowl, defeating Georgia Tech to finish 9-2-1, setting up Young, Herrmann and all the rest for an unprecedented run of success over the next few seasons.

September 22, 1979

No. 17 Purdue 28, No. 5 Notre Dame 22—Bounce Back for the Carmel Connection

Fresh off a 9-2-1 season, the 1979 Boilermakers had high hopes. A week one win over Wisconsin helped the squad climb to no. 5 in the AP Poll in advance of a road trip to UCLA. It all came apart on a steamy night in Los Angeles as the Bruins dominated the first half, knocked Herrmann out of the game early in the second half and held on for a 31–21 upset. It wouldn't get easier for the Boilermakers as they returned home to face 5th-ranked Notre Dame.

The Irish were fresh off an upset of Michigan in their opener and looking for a second straight road win over a ranked foe. More than 70,500 people showed up on the sun-splashed afternoon, the largest crowd to ever take in a football game in the state at the time. They saw an even game early, as the Irish scored first but Herrmann hit Dave Young for a 15-yard touchdown; the game was 7–7 after one.

The Irish led 13–7 at the half, thanks to a pair of field goals, and then extended their lead to 20–7 in the third quarter. Purdue responded with a scoring drive to cut the deficit in half when halfback Wally Jones took a pitch through the left side of the offensive line on third-and-goal from the 1. On Notre Dame's ensuing drive, the "Junk Defense" stepped up and made play when cornerback Marcus McKinnie made an interception on third down and returned the ball inside the Irish 10-yard line. Jones scored on a 3-yard run on the final play of the third quarter, and the Boilermakers took a 21–20 lead.

Herrmann had one more touchdown drive in him, connecting with former high school teammate Bart Burrell for a 6-yard score midway through the quarter to extend the lead to 28–20. The famed "Carmel Connection" had produced what would end up being the decisive score. The defense—with Tom Kingsbury, Kevin Motts and Keena Turner leading the attack—kept the Irish offense from threatening the rest of the way. Notre Dame's final 2 points came on a safety when a high snap forced punter Joe Linville to cover a punt in the end zone, saving a potential disaster in the closing minutes.

With that win, Purdue's season was right back on track. The following Monday, they shot right back into the Top 10.

NOVEMBER 10, 1979

NO. 14 PURDUE 24, NO. 10 MICHIGAN 21—TOPPLING TOP 10 WOLVERINES

Following an early October loss at Minnesota that left Purdue 3-2 overall, 1-1 in conference play, the Boilermakers reeled off four straight wins. The home victories against Illinois and Northwestern and road wins at Michigan State and Iowa weren't always pretty. In fact, three of the four contests were decided by a touchdown or less. But when the dust settled, the Old Gold and Black were 7-2 and 5-1 with two games to go.

They would close the season at Indiana, which would be no easy task. But before that Bucket showdown would come another major challenge in the form of no. 10 Michigan coming to Ross-Ade Stadium.

Bo Schembechler's Wolverines were in the thick of the Big Ten title hunt as well. A win over Purdue and an upset of Ohio State in the final week of the season would get Michigan to its second consecutive Rose Bowl. Nearly seventy thousand saw the home team dominate the first half of play, with the "Junk Defense" recovering three fumbles, grabbing two interceptions and blocking a punt. Purdue held Michigan to just 67 yards in the first half, and the Wolverines converted just one third-down attempt in seven chances. But at the break, Purdue's lead was just 7–0.

The second half began with another Purdue defensive stop, and when Michigan had a bad snap on the punt, Purdue took over at the Michigan 25. Herrmann shocked everyone in attendance with a quarterback sneak for the score, just his second rushing touchdown in three years as Purdue's starter, and the home team led 14–0.

On the next possession, junior defensive back Bill Kay came up with his third interception of the day, but the offense again failed to convert the turnover into points. Michigan finally got on the board with a sustained touchdown drive, but a missed PAT left the score at 14–6 after three.

Purdue kicker John Seibel added a 29-yard field goal early in the fourth quarter to extend the lead to 17–6. Another interception led to a rushing touchdown by Benny McCall, his second of the day, and Purdue found itself up 24–6 with just over ten minutes remaining. Future All-American Anthony Carter jump-started the Wolverines by returning the ensuing kickoff to midfield. Michigan scored a few plays later, although a two-point try failed, leaving the score 24–12 with just over eight minutes remaining.

Quarterback Mark Herrmann led one of college football's most prolific offenses while at Purdue, leading the Boilermakers to thirty-three wins. *Purdue Athletics.*

Michigan's onside kick failed, but they achieved the same result moments later when McCall fumbled near midfield. Six plays later, Butch Woolfork scored, and the lead was now 24–19. Herrmann drove the Boilermakers to midfield before throwing his only interception of the day on a tipped ball. With three minutes remaining, in a game the Boilermakers had dominated in every aspect, Michigan was now just 27 yards from stealing a win.

After picking up 3 yards on first down, Michigan gained 15 more yards on a screen pass. That gave them a fresh set of downs at the Purdue 10-yard line. Two unsuccessful pass plays led to third-and-goal. Quarterback Rick Wangler scrambled for 8 yards, bringing up fourth-and-goal from the 2. Schembechler called a triple-option, and the defensive front could not have played it more perfectly, with every man executing his assignment before linebacker James Looney dropped Wangler for an 8-yard loss.

The Boilermakers took a strategic safety in the final minute of play, but Michigan would not threaten again, with the final score 24–21. The Boilermakers defeated Indiana the following weekend, earning an invitation to the Bluebonnet Bowl in Houston, where they handled Tennessee and secured the first ten-win season in program history.

1980s
MOMENTS OF GREATNESS

CAMPBELL, EVERETT AND WOODSON

November 8, 1980

No. 17 Purdue 58, Iowa 13—Herrmann Hammers Hawkeyes

Expectations were sky high for the Boilermakers in 1980. Senior quarterback Mark Herrmann was back and closing in on the NCAA record for career passing yards. The team was ranked ninth in the preseason AP Poll and expected to challenge Michigan and Ohio State for the Big Ten title. The Boilermakers then dropped two of the season's first three games and fell out of the polls completely.

Five straight wins got the Boilermakers back on track as they welcomed Iowa to town in early November. The Hawkeyes were 3-5 and in the middle of the pack in the Big Ten under second-year head coach Hayden Fry. They were simply no match for the home team.

The potent Purdue offense scored on nine of its first eleven possessions to run up a 51–7 advantage before Coach Jim Young elected to play his reserves for the fourth quarter. Three first-half field goals were all that kept the game from being a real laugher, but the Boilermakers broke it open with 28 points in the third quarter.

Herrmann had a game for the ages, completing 26 of 34 for 439 yards and three scores. The yardage total set the Purdue single-game record and was also the most passing yards in Big Ten history until Illinois quarterback Dave Wilson threw for 621 yards later that afternoon in a loss to Ohio State. Herrmann also became the NCAA career leader in pass attempts

Coach Jim Young and quarterback Mark Herrmann were a match made in heaven, with Herrmann ending his career as the NCAA's all-time passing leader. *Purdue Athletics.*

that day, but he wasn't the only Boilermaker making history. Tight end Dave Young caught eight passes for 143 yards and two scores and in the process became the Big Ten's all-time leader in receptions. Kicker Rick Anderson converted all seven PATs to set a Ross-Ade record while also booting three field goals; the 58 points put up by the home team broke the stadium scoring record as well.

The offense rolled up 607 yards on the day, second most in school history, and amassed more than 500 yards of total offense for the fourth straight game. They scored 50-plus for the second straight game after putting 52 on the board at Northwestern the previous week. Not to be left out, the defense forced seven turnovers, with cornerback Bill Kay leading the way returning an interception 75 yards for a score in the third quarter. It was as dominant a win as Ross-Ade had ever seen, and after the game even Hayden Fry was on board the Herrmann-for-Heisman train.

November 22, 1980

Purdue 24, Indiana 23—McCall and Marks to the Rescue

After falling short against Michigan with a shot at the Big Ten title the previous week, Purdue welcomed Indiana for the final game of the 1980 season. It was Senior Day for one of the most accomplished groups ever to wear the Old Gold and Black, including offensive stars like Herrmann, Young, Burrell, Quinn, Macon and McCall, as well as "Junk Defense" veterans like Kingsbury, Kay and Marks. And while the Old Oaken Bucket was on the line, some drama was missing, as the Boilermakers had already accepted a bid to play Missouri in the Liberty Bowl.

A record crowd of more than seventy-one thousand saw the road team dominate early. The Hoosiers led 10–0 after an early field goal and a second-quarter touchdown run. The record-breaking Purdue offense, after being shut out at Michigan, managed just a field goal in the final minute of the first half, trailing 10–3 at the break. Herrmann threw for a paltry 71 yards in the opening half. He would make up for it in his final thirty minutes inside Ross-Ade.

The first play of the third quarter was a 30-yard pass to receiver Steve Bryant. Less than five minutes into the second half, Purdue had tied the game with running back Benny McCall covering the final yard for the score. After a missed Indiana field goal, Herrmann led a six-play, 80-yard drive that ended with one more Carmel Connection to receiver Bart Burrell. Purdue led 17–10 after three.

The Hoosiers caught a break when Jimmy Smith fumbled out the back of the end zone to give IU the ball at the 20-yard line. Moments later, they caught another when Purdue was called for roughing the kicker, keeping a stalled drive alive. Finally, Indiana tied it up with a short TD run. Purdue once again drove the length of the field to take the lead. This time, Herrmann needed seven plays to go 80 yards, capped off by a gutsy decision from Coach Young. Facing fourth-and-inches from inside the 5-yard line, Young passed on a short field goal that would have given the Boilermakers the lead. Instead, McCall took a sweep around the right end and hit pay dirt, putting the home team up 24–17.

Another Smith fumble gave Indiana one last chance with just over six minutes remaining. Fifteen plays and 65 yards later, IU scored on a 10-yard pass play on fourth down to pull within one, 24–23. Coach Lee Corso elected to go for the win with a two-point try. Quarterback Tim Clifford dropped back and looked for his tight end dragging across the field just inside the goal line. Senior linebacker Mike Marks undercut the pass and dove, deflecting it to the turf to maintain the lead.

With seconds remaining and the home crowd already starting to celebrate in the north end zone, Indiana recovered an onside kick. The Hoosiers lined up for a 59-yard field goal to win, but Marks burst through the line and tipped the kick, causing it to fall well short and preserving the victory.

Herrmann was nearly perfect in the second half, completing 13 of 14 (his lone incompletion came from an offensive pass interference call) for 252 yards and a score. He also became the first Boilermaker signal caller since Bob Griese to beat IU three straight times. It was a fitting end to a Hall of Fame career, although on this day, there was plenty of credit to go around.

SEPTEMBER 12, 1981

PURDUE 27, NO. 19 STANFORD 19—JIMMY SMITH PLAYS THE HERO

The 1981 season opener was full of uncertainty for the Boilermakers. It was the first game in four years without Mark Herrmann running the offense. There were a lot of pieces needing to be replaced on both sides of the ball after the graduation of one of the most successful classes in program history. To make matters worse, they would be facing a Top 20 Stanford team led by junior quarterback John Elway.

The game, with the Goodyear Blimp floating high above Ross-Ade and a national viewing audience thanks to ABC broadcasting the game, was exciting from the start. Stanford scored on their opening drive, but momentum swung wildly back in favor of the Boilermakers when Jimmy Smith returned the ensuing kickoff 100 yards for a score. A missed PAT left the Cardinals on top, 7–6. Smith scored again late in the first on a 1-yard run to put the home team up 13–7.

Stanford added a pair of field goals in the second quarter, the latter a Ross-Ade-record 59-yard boot. But Smith scored his second rushing touchdown, and third overall, late in the half to keep the Boilermakers ahead 20–13 at the break.

Elway finally connected on a touchdown pass in the third quarter, hooking up with running back Vince White. The PAT was blocked, however, leaving the Boilermakers on top, 20–19. Sophomore quarterback

Halfback Jimmy Smith goes in for one of his two scores in the upset win over John Elway and no. 19 Stanford. *Purdue Athletics.*

Scott Campbell struck quickly on the next Purdue possession, leading a six-play, 74-yard scoring drive, capped off by a 29-yard touchdown pass to Steve Bryant.

Stanford drove to the Purdue 2-yard line on their next possession and looked poised to score when the Cardinal fullback fumbled into the end zone and safety Tim Seneff recovered for a touchback. Purdue turned the ball over two plays later, giving Stanford a second life. But the defense came up big once again as defensive back Robert Williams recovered another fumble to preserve the win.

On the day, Elway completed 33 of 44 for 418 yards and a score, but it wasn't enough. The Purdue defense forced three red zone turnovers in the second half and turned away the Cardinals a fourth time as the clock expired to clinch the victory. Smith, the senior running back for the Boilermakers, finished with twenty-seven carries for 91 yards and the two rushing touchdowns to go with the longest kick return in Ross-Ade history.

SEPTEMBER 26, 1981

PURDUE 15, NO. 13 NOTRE DAME 14—LAST-SECOND HEROICS FOR CAMPBELL

After the season-opening win over Stanford, the Boilermakers lost a heartbreaker at Minnesota, 16–13. They returned home in week three to take on 13th-ranked Notre Dame. The Irish had just fallen to Michigan the previous week, losing their no. 1 ranking in the process. First-year head coach Gerry Faust was hoping to right the ship against the Boilermakers.

More than seventy thousand people packed Ross-Ade to see what ended up being a defensive struggle. Notre Dame got on the board late in the second quarter and held a 7–0 lead at the half. Sophomore quarterback Scott Campbell led an eight-play, 66-yard scoring drive midway through the third to tie the game at 7–7, with Wally Jones doing the honors from a yard out.

Notre Dame went back on top after running back Phil Carter covered 50 yards on three plays, the final a 30-yard sprint to the end zone to put the Irish up 14–7 with less than three minutes remaining. Things were about to get wild.

On second down from his own 29, Campbell connected with running back Eric Jordan for 28 yards to midfield. After a Notre Dame timeout and an incomplete pass, Campbell took the snap and scrambled to his right under pressure. He began to take off toward the line of scrimmage and then threw a missile toward the end zone. George Pickens was wide open at the goal line, but the ball was falling short. Luckily, Steve Bryant was streaking toward the ball, and he snatched it out of the air before stepping out of bounds at the 1-yard line. On first-and-goal, Jones was thrown for a 6-yard loss, and two Campbell passes fell incomplete, bringing up fourth-and-goal with twenty-three seconds remaining.

After a timeout, Steve Bryant lined up wide left. He went in motion to the right and then planted his foot at the snap and sprinted back to his left. Campbell took the shotgun snap and laid a perfect pass over Bryant's outside shoulder for the touchdown. Head Coach Jim Young immediately elected to go for the win with a two-point conversion. Shockingly, the Boilermakers called the same play on the opposite side of the field. This time, Bryant lined up wide right, motioned left and then sprinted back right. Campbell's pass was just out of the reach of the defender's outstretched hand, and Bryant held on tight for the win, 15–14.

Defensive back Tim Seneff intercepted a desperation throw from the Irish, and the celebration began, with students swarming the field with six seconds remaining on the clock. They cleared the field enough for Campbell to take one more snap to run out the clock. Then the party started back up again and lasted well into the night.

October 6, 1984

Purdue 28, No. 2 Ohio State 23—Woodson and Everett Shock the Buckeyes

The 1984 season began with a bang as the Boilermakers upset no. 8 Notre Dame in the Hoosier Dome dedication game. They returned home for a showdown with defending national champion Miami in week two and fell to the 5th-ranked Hurricanes. The Boilermakers then opened Big Ten play with wins against Minnesota and at Michigan State to stand at 3-1 when they welcomed their third Top 10 opponent to town in no. 2 Ohio State.

The Buckeyes were perfect on the year, averaging more than 36 points per game, and featured no fewer than five future All-Americans, including receiver Cris Carter and running back Keith Byars. It would be a tall task for the home team.

The Boilermakers got on the board first when junior quarterback Jim Everett found Steve Griffin for a 20-yard score in the first quarter, but the Buckeyes answered with a touchdown run by Byars to make it 7–7 after one. OSU added a field goal in the second to lead 10–7 at the half. Byars scored again early in the third quarter, and the Boilermakers trailed by 10.

The teams traded punts before Purdue turned the tide. On first down from their own 35, a run play was called in from the sideline, but Everett saw the defense was in man-to-man coverage and he liked Griffin's matchup. The offensive line picked up the Buckeye blitz, and Griffin's defender never stood a chance. Everett floated a perfect pass to the receiver running a post pattern toward the left sideline, and 65 yards later, the score was 17–14.

Defensive back Donnie Anderson ended Ohio State's next drive, intercepting quarterback Mike Tomczak at the 5-yard line and returning it out past the 30. On the next play, Everett hit receiver Rick Brunner for a 47-yard gain. The Boilermakers were knocking on the door as the fourth quarter began. Three plays into the final quarter, Everett hit fullback Bruce King on a play-action pass from 4 yards out to give the home team the lead, 21–17.

Quarterback Jim Everett had a lot of admirers while at Purdue, including former Boilermaker Neil Armstrong. *Purdue Athletics.*

The Buckeyes were moving the ball on their next possession, with Byars leading the way. But on third-and-long from near midfield, as Tomczak dropped back to pass, disaster struck. Sophomore free safety Rod Woodson got a perfect read on the throw, undercut the route to make the interception and sprinted 55 yards to the end zone for a 28–17 lead. The Buckeyes cut the lead to 5 with a Tomczak to Carter touchdown in the closing minutes, but the two-point try failed, as did the ensuing onside kick. Then the storming of Ross-Ade began.

Byars had one of the best games in stadium history with 191 rushing yards and 102 receiving yards to go with two touchdowns. But it wasn't enough to overcome Everett's near perfect day (17 of 23 for 257 yards and three scores) or Woodson's unbelievable performance (twenty tackles along with the 55-yard pick-six).

November 3, 1984

Purdue 31, Michigan 29—Clinching Unprecedented Three-for-Three

In the game of football, it is very hard to beat a great gameplan executed at a high level. That was the combination Purdue hit on when Michigan came to town in early November 1984. Offensively, the Boilermakers relied on high-percentage pass plays and pinpoint precision from their quarterback. On defense, it was a focus on assignment execution to stifle Michigan's potent option offense.

This combination led to a near-perfect first half for the home team and a shocking 24–0 lead for the Old Gold and Black. During the first half, quarterback Jim Everett completed 14 of 17 passes for 170 yards and two scores. He led touchdown drives of 97, 57 and 45 yards, along with another scoring drive that covered 74 yards before ending in a field goal.

Defensively, the Boilermakers were in every way equal to the offense, forcing four Michigan punts while surrendering just three first downs and 32 total yards. Michigan finally got on the board in the third quarter, but running back Rodney Carter scored midway through the fourth quarter to make it 31–7 Purdue.

A desperate Michigan offense put up a valiant comeback effort with 22 points in the final four minutes, aided by a successful onside kick and a touchdown with three seconds left in the game, but it wasn't enough. For the second time in less than a month, fans stormed the field. They were celebrating something never done before in nearly one hundred years of Purdue football. Coupled with the win three weeks earlier over Ohio State and the season-opening victory over Notre Dame in Indianapolis, it was the first time a Purdue team had slain all three giants in a single season.

November 17, 1984

Purdue 31, Indiana 24—Carter Carries Boilermakers to Bucket Win

Strange things can happen during rivalry games, and the 1984 edition of the battle for the Old Oaken Bucket was no different. The Boilermakers headed into the final week of the season trying to block out the disappointment of the previous week. Purdue dropped a game to Wisconsin in Madison that turned out to be of vital importance. A win over the Badgers would have put Purdue in a tie for first place in the Big Ten with Ohio State, whom the Boilermakers had beaten. Under that scenario, a win over IU would have clinched the program's second trip to the Rose Bowl.

Alas, it was not to be, with a 30–13 loss to the Badgers dashing those hopes. Instead, Purdue turned its attention to its in-state rival, which was in the midst of one of the worst seasons in program history. The Hoosiers came into the game 0-10 under first-year head coach Bill Mallory. Naturally, the visiting team jumped out to a 14–0 lead in the first quarter.

The Boilermakers were able to snap out of the early funk to put together a pair of scoring drives to pull even at the half, 14–14. They then took a 17–14 lead on a Mike Rendina field goal early in the third quarter, but the Hoosiers hit a triple of their own to make it 17–17 late in the third.

The Boilermakers drove 80 yards on the ensuing possession, with Everett diving in from the 1-yard line to cap it off. The defense got the ball right back

Running back Rodney Carter amassed 225 yards of offense and a score as the Boilermakers took out the Hoosiers and secured a trip to the Peach Bowl, November 17, 1984. *Purdue Athletics.*

with a three-and-out, forcing an Indiana punt. On third-and-long, Everett avoided a blitzing linebacker and zinged a beautiful pass to Steve Griffin at the goal line for a 27-yard scoring strike to put the home team up 31–17. The Hoosiers scored once more, but the lead was secure, as was the Bucket.

Everett finished with 265 yards and a touchdown and became the first quarterback in program history to surpass 3,000 passing yards in the regular season. But the real star of the day was running back Rodney Carter. The junior from New Jersey carried the ball twenty-two times for 148 yards and a score while also catching four passes for 77 yards.

After the game, Boilermakers accepted a bid to the Peach Bowl, where they lost a heartbreaker to Virginia, 27–24. It would be more than a decade before the Old Gold and Black returned to the postseason, when Joe Tiller, the defensive coordinator for Leon Burtnett on the 1984 squad, returned to West Lafayette and led the squad to the Alamo Bowl in his first season at the helm.

October 12, 1985

Purdue 30, Illinois 24—Everett Outduels Trudeau

"Three yards and a cloud of dust" was an offensive mindset made popular by Ohio State legend Woody Hayes, but in the mid-'80s, it could have described the mindset of Big Ten football in general. Half of the league's teams had more rushing yards than passing yards in 1984, including powerhouse programs Michigan and Ohio State. The nearly sixty-nine thousand fans who packed Ross-Ade Stadium to see Purdue play Illinois in October 1985 saw the exact opposite of that.

Illinois signal caller Jack Trudeau got the visitors on the board first with a 6-yard scoring pass to All-American receiver David Williams, but Jim Everett answered with an 11-yard score to Ray Wallace. The Boilermakers took a 13–10 lead at the half on Everett's second touchdown pass of the day. In the second quarter alone, Everett was 13 of 17 for 208 yards.

The third quarter saw Everett connect with Mark "Turf" Jackson for a 64-yard scoring pass, Jackson's second of the day, to give the Boilermakers a 20–10 lead. Trudeau and Williams connected again for the Illini to cut the lead to 20–17, but a Purdue field goal and an 18-yard scoring pass from Everett to Steve Griffin made it 30–17 with less than ten minutes remaining.

Fans were treated to an offensive explosion as Illinois quarterback Jack Trudeau threw for 413 yards, only to see Jim Everett pass for 464 yards and four touchdowns in the Purdue win. *Purdue Athletics.*

Trudeau and Williams connected for a third score with just over two minutes remaining to make it 30–24. The Illini forced a Purdue punt and took over at midfield with less than two minutes remaining. But Rod Woodson came up huge on a fourth-down play, knocking the ball out of Williams's hands inside the 5-yard line, and the Purdue offense took over. Boilermakers win.

When the smoke cleared from the shootout for the Purdue Cannon, the Boilermakers stood victorious. Everett finished 27 of 47 for a career-best 464 yards and four scores. Trudeau, was nearly as prolific for the visitors, finishing with a career-high 413 yards and three scores. At the time, those two passing performances both ranked in the top eleven all-time passing games in Big Ten history. Illinois receiver David Williams finished with sixteen catches for 164 yards and three scores for the Illini, while Rodney Carter (eleven catches, 158 yards) and Turf Jackson (six catches, 140 yards) both went over the century mark for Purdue. It was an aerial game for the ages and a sign of things to come, for college football and in West Lafayette.

November 22, 1986

Purdue 17, Indiana 15—Woodson's Masterpiece

Every so often in sports, an individual's performance is so transformative that it overtakes the game itself. That was the case on Senior Day in 1986 when Rod Woodson went from being a Purdue great to being in the conversation for the greatest ever.

The game itself was not an epic matchup, with the Hoosiers coming in at 6-4 while the Boilermakers were 2-8 on the year. Head Coach Leon Burtnett had resigned three weeks earlier and would be coaching his final game after five years at the helm.

The afternoon started with a bang as the Boilermakers went through pregame warmups in black jerseys. Then they were surprised by their head coach upon returning to the locker room just before kickoff. Burtnett had his staff distribute gold jerseys with an Old Oaken Bucket patch on the arm, the first time Purdue would wear gold in a game since the 1940s.

The game itself ended on a thrilling high note as well, as sophomore defensive lineman Scott Schult blocked a 34-yard field goal attempt by Indiana kicker Pete Stoyanovich with less than a minute to go to preserve

Running back Rod Woodson takes a pitch and looks for a hole. On the day, Woodson had fifteen carries for 95 yards and caught three passes for 67 yards. *Purdue Athletics.*

Woodson takes a knee in his special Bucket edition gold jersey. Defensively, Woodson had ten tackles and a forced fumble while he also returned five kicks or punts for a total of 76 yards. *Purdue Athletics.*

the 17–15 Purdue win. James Medlock and Calvin Williams accounted for Purdue's two touchdowns on the day, while Jonathan Briggs added the all-important field goal. But the game belonged to Woodson.

Not only did the senior from Fort Wayne play virtually every down at his regular cornerback position on defense, but he also played the majority of the offensive snaps for Purdue. The three-time Big Ten Champion hurdler also returned kicks and punts while playing on various other special teams units.

On the day, Woodson had ten tackles, a forced fumble and a pass break up on defense; carried the ball fifteen times for 95 yards out of the backfield; caught three passes for 67 yards at receiver; returned three punts for 30 yards; and had two kickoff returned for 46 yards. He was also alongside Schult on the blocked field goal, recovering the loose ball and sprinting to the end zone for what was thought to be a clinching touchdown, leading to one of the greatest dogpile celebrations imaginable in the north end zone. Alas, the score was called back due to penalty, but the result remained the same. The legendary tale of Rod Woodson, Purdue's last sixty-minute man, was born.

1990s

THROUGH THE WILDERNESS

ALSTOTT, COLVIN AND TILLER

September 12, 1992

Purdue 41, No. 17 California 14—Blowing Out the Bears

Heading into the 1992 season, hopes were not high for Purdue fans. Head Coach Jim Colletto was in year two of a rebuilding project that had seen the program go nearly a decade without a winning season. And to top it off, the season opener would be against a Top 20 opponent in the California Golden Bears. The Boilermakers responded to the skeptics by playing a perfect half of football.

Cal received the opening kickoff and then fumbled on the game's second play from scrimmage. It took the Purdue offense just three plays to cover 40 yards, with running back Jeff Hill getting his first score of the day. A field goal and an 11-yard touchdown run by Earl Coleman found the home team up 17–0 after one.

Cal finally got on the board with a field goal early in the second quarter, but sophomore quarterback Matt Pike threw an 8-yard scoring pass to Hill on the next drive to make it 24–3. Linebacker Romond Batten got an interception on the next Cal drive leading to a 1-yard scoring run by Arlee Conners to make it 31–3. Defensive back Tank Adams intercepted another Cal pass in the final minute of the first half, setting up Conners's second scoring run of the day; at the half, Purdue led 38–3.

Both teams added a field goal in the third quarter and Cal scored a meaningless touchdown late, but the game was long over by halftime. On the day, the defense forced six turnovers, and the offense played a fundamentally sound brand of football, rushing for 162 yards and throwing for 144 yards. More importantly, they committed zero turnovers and took advantage of every Cal miscue to earn the program's first win over a ranked opponent since taking out no. 2 Ohio State in 1984.

November 21, 1992

Purdue 13, Indiana 10—Jimmy Young to the Rescue

A lot more was on the line for Indiana than for Purdue in the 1992 Bucket game. The Hoosiers came in with a 5-5 record, hoping to secure a winning season and a second straight bowl bid. The Boilermakers were 3-7 on the season and playing for little more than pride. Turns out pride can be a heck of a motivator.

On his Senior Day, quarterback Eric Hunter was the star of the day for the Boilermakers, rushing for 117 yards, including a game-winning 21-yard score in the fourth quarter while passing for 163 yards. Purdue gained nearly 200 yards more in total offense while securing ten more first downs than the Hoosiers on the day.

Purdue blocked a punt in the second quarter, setting the offense up with first-and-goal from the 4, but the Boilermakers were forced to settle for a field goal for the only points in the first half. The teams traded field goals in the third quarter, and the Hoosiers took their first lead of the day on a 2-yard bootleg touchdown run by quarterback Trent Green. The Boilermakers responded with a twelve-play, 69-yard drive that ended with Hunter's 21-yard scoring dash to put the home team back on top, 13–10.

Green had one more chance to win the game for the Hoosiers. He took the Indiana offense on an eighteen-play drive to the Purdue 5-yard line. But on the nineteenth play of the drive, Green made a fatal mistake, throwing an interception to junior cornerback Jimmy Young in the end zone. Young took off downfield, only green grass (and Green, the quarterback) in front of him. Green dove for Young and grabbed him by the facemask, throwing the Boilermaker to the ground, earning Green an ejection and starting a brief skirmish on the sidelines.

Hunter came out and took a knee, running out the clock and starting the party. As jubilant fans mobbed the field, the Boilermakers celebrated with the Bucket for the first time in three seasons.

OCTOBER 8, 1994

PURDUE 49, MINNESOTA 37—ALSTOTT ALL EVERYTHING VS. MINNESOTA

A big question around West Lafayette during the 1994 and 1995 seasons was: "Can a fullback win the Heisman Trophy?" The fullback in question, of course, was Mike Alstott, and despite the answer eventually being a resounding no from the Downtown Athletic Club, it wasn't for a lack of trying. Had Alstott been able to play Minnesota each week, that answer might have been different. In 1993, Alstott had his best game to date in a loss to the Gophers, rushing for 171 yards and tying the school record with five touchdowns in the game.

The 1994 version of the rivalry found the Boilermakers off to a hot start, coming in at 3-1 overall and fresh from a road win at no. 25 Illinois. The Gophers were 2-3 and hoping to right the ship after road losses at Indiana and Kansas State.

The Gophers jumped out to a 17–7 lead, a 9-yard scoring run by Corey Rogers being the only bright spot for the Boilermakers early. Alstott broke a

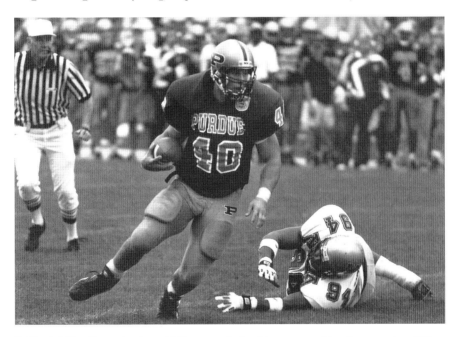

Fullback Mike Alstott dominated Minnesota during his career, rushing for more than 500 yards and thirteen touchdowns in four games against the Gophers. *Purdue Athletics.*

38-yard scoring run midway through the second quarter to make it 17–14. Each team scored again before intermission to make it 24–21 Minnesota as defense appeared to be optional.

The Gophers got a field goal early in the third, but a pair of rushing touchdowns by Alstott and Edwin Watson put Purdue up 35–27 headed to the fourth quarter. Minnesota scored early in the final stanza and converted a two-point try to make it 35–35. That's when Alstott broke the game wide open.

On second-and-7 from near midfield, Alstott took a handoff and headed toward right tackle. He cut back across the grain after reaching the second level of the Minnesota defense, broke one tackle and was gone for a 48-yard scoring run. Alstott would add a fourth touchdown run late in the fourth to put the game on ice.

For the day, the A-Train ran for a career-best 183 yards on twenty-five carries to lead his team to victory. In his four career games against the Gophers, Alstott finished with 517 yards rushing and thirteen touchdowns. It was the only team he ever broke the century mark against three times in his Purdue career.

November 4, 1995

Purdue 38, Wisconsin 27—Alstott Bowls Over the Badgers

During his amazing career at Purdue, Mike Alstott rushed for more than 100 yards in a game sixteen different times. However, he broke the 200-yard mark just twice—in the final game of his career when he ran for 264 yards at Indiana and three weeks earlier when he put up 204 in a win over Wisconsin.

Big plays were the order of the day for the Purdue offense as Brian Alford started things off with a 64-yard touchdown catch from quarterback Rick Trefzger. Later in the first, Edwin Watson burst loose for a 63-yard scoring run, and the Boilermakers led 14–7 after one. Alstott got in on the action with a 40-yard touchdown run in the opening moments of the second quarter, and the home team led 20–14 at the break.

Wisconsin took a 1-point lead following a Trefzger fumble, but Watson scored his second of the day; the Boilermakers converted a two-point try to make up for a missed PAT in the first half. Purdue led 28–21 heading into the fourth.

Brad Bobich added a field goal to extend the Purdue lead to 10 early in the fourth, but Wisconsin hit right back with a 54-yard touchdown pass to make it a one-score game again. The Boilermakers responded with a twelve-play, 66-yard scoring drive with Alstott crashing in from 2 yards out to put the game out of reach.

On the day, the senior fullback from Joliet, Illinois, finished with 204 yards on thirty-six carries. His two touchdowns pulled him clear of the great Leroy Keyes to become Purdue's all-time scoring leader, and he became just the sixth Boilermaker to ever rush for 200-plus yards in a game. But he didn't do it alone. Watson finished with 194 yards on twenty-one carries as the offense amassed 596 yards on the day. The 398 combined rushing yards for Watson and Alstott remains the program record for rushing yards by two teammates in Purdue history two decades later.

OCTOBER 5, 1996

PURDUE 30, MINNESOTA 27—MINNESOTA THRILLER…AGAIN

Sometimes two football programs, for a time, can be very closely matched. That was the case for Purdue and Minnesota in the late 1980s and early 1990s. Heading into the 1996 battle in Ross-Ade, six of the previous nine meetings were decided by 4 points or less. That included a 59–56 Minnesota win in 1993 and a 39–38 Gopher victory in 1995.

The 1996 version of the rivalry would indeed prove to be more of the same. The Boilermakers got on the board first when free safety Derrick Brown intercepted a deflected Gopher pass and returned it 59 yards for a score on Minnesota's first possession. The Gophers scored the next 16 points unanswered until receiver Brian Alford caught a 42-yard touchdown from quarterback John Reeves to make it 16–14. Minnesota gave the ball back when a bad snap led to a terrible punt and a very short field for Purdue. Running back Kendall Matthews scored two plays later to retake the lead.

On the Gophers' next possession, Brown again came up with another interception, setting up a second touchdown for Matthews. The reserve running back was pushed into action when starter Edwin Watson aggravated a knee injury early in the game. The junior from St. Charles, Missouri, made the most of his opportunity, carrying the ball thirty times for 131 yards and a pair of touchdowns on the day.

Kicker Chris Arnce added a 37-yard field goal for the only points in the third quarter as the Boilermakers extended the lead to 30–19. Minnesota found the end zone midway through the fourth quarter and converted a two-point try to pull within 3. The Gophers got the ball back one last time, needing a field goal to tie. They reached midfield, but the Purdue defense stiffened and forced a turnover on downs.

In the end, it was another game between the Gophers and the Boilermakers decided by less than a touchdown.

NOVEMBER 9, 1996

PURDUE 9, NO. 9 MICHIGAN 3—BOILERMAKERS RESPOND TO COLLETTO QUITTING

On the Monday morning before Purdue was set to welcome Top 10 Michigan to town, Head Coach Jim Colletto shocked the world. With three games left in the season, he resigned. The sixth-year head coach had compiled a 20-40-3 record in his time at the helm. His departure didn't come as a surprise to many Purdue fans. It remained to be seen how it would play out with the team.

The Boilermaker defense was up to the task early, shutting out the Wolverines in the first half while forcing two Michigan fumbles. A 28-yard field goal by Shane Ryan was the only scoring in the opening thirty minutes and put Purdue in a great spot. Michigan tied the game with a short field goal of its own early in the third quarter, and the game headed to the fourth all knotted up, 3–3.

The defense continued to pester the Wolverines, with linebacker Chris Koeppen stripping Michigan quarterback Scott Dreisbach and recovering the fumble to give his offense a chance. On the ensuing possession, they rode that wave of momentum. Senior quarterback Rick Trefzger evaded the Michigan rush and scrambled to his left, releasing a pass to Brian Alford just as the defense caught up to him. Alford put the clamps on the pass in the end zone, a 5-yard score, to give Purdue the 9–3 lead.

The Boilermakers intercepted Dreisbach to end Michigan's final two drives of the day, accounting for five total turnovers in the victory. Koeppen tied a school record with two fumble recoveries on the day while leading the way with ten tackles. Chike Okeafor added nine tackles and a forced a fumble. They held the Wolverines to fewer than 300 yards of total offense and just 56 rushing yards.

Colletto would lose his final two games at Purdue, falling to Northwestern and Indiana to close out his head coaching career. Three weeks after the season was over, he was named the offensive coordinator at Notre Dame. But Purdue fans would spend little time missing their lost coach, for he was about to be replaced by a legend.

September 13, 1997

Purdue 28, No. 12 Notre Dame 17—Tiller Gets First Career Win

The Joe Tiller era began with a thud in the fall of 1997. The Boilermakers actually opened the season on the road, in Tiller's home town of Toledo, Ohio. He had nearly one hundred family and friends in attendance to celebrate the occasion but saw his team fall short, losing to the Rockets 36–22. Week two didn't figure to get any easier with no. 12 Notre Dame coming to Ross-Ade for the home opener.

As if the Boilermakers needed any additional motivation, Tiller's predecessor, Jim Colletto, would be on the visitor's sideline, calling plays for

Senior quarterback Billy Dicken took advantage of his one year under Coach Tiller, throwing for 3,100 yards and twenty-one touchdowns while leading Purdue to nine wins. *Purdue Athletics.*

the Irish. Notre Dame had won eleven straight in the series, with Purdue's last victory over the Irish coming in 1985.

A sellout crowd of more than sixty-eight thousand saw the Boilermakers get on the board first when quarterback Billy Dicken led an eleven-play, 99-yard scoring drive, capped off by running back Edwin Watson's 1-yard dive through the middle of the line for the 7–0 lead. Watson accounted for 68 total yards on the drive. He added another scoring run in the second quarter, and the Boilermakers led 14–10 at the half.

After a scoreless third quarter, the home team still clinging to the lead, the Boilermaker defense got on the board. With the Irish near midfield, pressure forced quarterback Ron Powlus out of the pocket. As defensive end Rosevelt Colvin dove to tackle the Irish QB, he forced a fumble. Defensive back Adrian Beasley scooped up the loose ball and sprinted 43 yards for a touchdown to put Purdue up 21–10.

Notre Dame found the end zone with less than two minutes remaining but a failed onside kick gave the Boilermakers the ball at midfield with just 1:47 standing between them and the upset. The Irish used their final timeout

Coach Joe Tiller, standing next to freshman quarterback Drew Brees, celebrates his first win as the leader of the Boilermakers. *Purdue Athletics.*

Fans stormed the field following the program's first win over Notre Dame since 1985.
Purdue Athletics.

after a 2-yard run by Kendall Matthews. On second down, Tiller bucked
conventional wisdom by calling his signature bubble screen. Dicken hit
freshman receiver Vinny Sutherland, who sprinted down to the 3-yard line
before being tackled. Matthews scored on the next play as the Boilermakers
put the finishing touches on the upset.

Dicken finished the day 26 of 39 for 352 yards, the first of five 300-plus-
yard games for the senior quarterback in 1997. Defensive back Lee Brush
tied linebacker Willie Fells for the lead in tackles with a dozen each, while
Lamar Conard and Mike Rose had eleven tackles apiece. As the clock
reached zero, tens of thousands of fans stormed the field, overtaking Tiller
in the middle of his postgame interview with ABC's Jack Arute. Through
the mayhem, Tiller seemed prophetic. "I hope we have a whole lot more of
these," he yelled into the mic. "It's a great win for Purdue. The first of many,
we hope." Indeed, it was.

NOVEMBER 8, 1997

NO. 23 PURDUE 22, MICHIGAN STATE 21—COLVIN CLUTCH IN MICHIGAN STATE MIRACLE

After the win over Notre Dame in week two, the Boilermakers ripped off five more, clinching a winning season and bowl eligibility in October. A setback at Iowa left Purdue at 6-2 when Michigan State came to town. The Spartans were 5-3 and reeling after dropping three straight.

MSU led 14–7 at the half before a short Shane Ryan field goal pulled the Boilermakers to within 4 early in the fourth quarter. The Spartans extended their lead with a 65-yard touchdown pass less than two minutes later to go up 21–10. That's where things stood with three minutes to go in the game.

MSU had an eleven-point lead and the ball, hoping to salt away the win. Facing fourth-and-15 from the 22-yard line with just 2:13 showing on the clock, MSU head coach Nick Saban called for a field goal. In a timeout just before the play, defensive coordinator Brock Spack told his unit that he had seen the future. One of them was going to block the kick, and another was going to scoop it up and score.

At the snap, defensive tackle Leo Perez slipped between two Spartans, took two steps and threw his right hand skyward, deflecting the kick and sending it directly behind the kicker. As if knowing that's where he needed to be, defensive end Rosevelt Colvin was there, all alone, two steps from the ball. He scooped it and sprinted 62 yards to pay dirt, making it 21–16 MSU. Even after a failed two-point conversion, the Boilermakers had a sliver of hope. Now they needed another miracle.

Lining up for the onside kick, kicker Chris Arnce drove the ball 5 yards down field before it took a high hop and then bounced a second time while two Spartans stood and stared at the ball. Their hesitation allowed receiver Chris Daniels to snatch it out of the air. Just under two minutes remained, and quarterback Billy Dicken trotted onto the field. Dicken had been benched earlier in the fourth quarter for freshman Drew Brees, but Brees threw an interception on his only drive of the game. Coach Joe Tiller figured that the senior gave him his best chance.

Needing to drive 55 yards in less than two minutes, Dicken fired a 16-yard pass to Brian Alford to move the chains. Edwin Watson made a one-handed grab on the next play for a 4-yard gain before running out of bounds to stop the clock. Next, Dicken connected with Donald

Defensive end Rosevelt Colvin was one of many heroes in the improbable comeback win over Michigan State, returning a blocked field goal for a fourth-quarter touchdown. *Purdue Athletics.*

Winston down the seam for another first down at the 18-yard line. Dicken then fired a bullet to Gabe Cox on a slant route, and Cox made it to the 4-yard line before going down. Timeout, Boilermakers, with 1:10 showing on the clock.

Coming out of the timeout, MSU got flagged for having twelve men on the field, moving the ball to the 2-yard line. Dicken went nowhere on a draw play, and MSU took a timeout. On second down, a patient Watson took the handoff and waited for a hole to develop, finally crossing the goal line to put Purdue up 22–21. Another two-point try failed, and Michigan State missed a long field goal on the final play as one of the most improbable victories in Ross-Ade history was secured.

SEPTEMBER 12, 1998

PURDUE 21, RICE 19—BREES GETS FIRST WIN

Joe Tiller's first year ended with nine wins and an Alamo Bowl title. Hopes were certainly high for year two, but things got off to a rocky start when the team headed west for the season opener and fell 27–17 to USC. Sophomore quarterback Drew Brees didn't play poorly in his first career start—completing 30 of 52 passes for 248 yards, two scores and a pair of interceptions—but it wasn't enough to win.

Week two saw the Boilermakers return home for what should have been a less daunting challenge against Rice. It would be anything but easy. The Owls brought with them a spread-option rushing attack that was unlike anything the Boilermakers would face the rest of the season. They ran thirty-one more offensive plays than Purdue and outgained the Boilermakers by 61 yards, notched twenty-six first downs on the day to Purdue's seventeen and dominated the time of possession battle, holding the ball for two-thirds of the contest. With such limited time for his offense to operate, Tiller knew that they needed to take advantage of every opportunity.

Brees got the Boilermakers on the board in the first quarter with a rushing touchdown and found Gabe Cox for a 23-yard touchdown pass in the second stanza as Purdue took a 14–3 lead into the half, thanks in part to a blocked field goal by Rosevelt Colvin. The teams traded third-quarter touchdowns, and the Boilermakers carried a two-score lead into the fourth. Rice opened the final frame by going on a sixteen-play drive that took more than eight minutes off the clock and ended in a field goal, making the score 21–13.

The Boilermakers got the ball back, but three plays later, Brees tried to hit Vinny Sutherland with a pass in the right flat. The ball went to the turf, and Rice jumped on it. After initially ruling the pass incomplete, the officials changed the ruling, saying that it was a lateral pass and a fumble, recovered by the Owls. Rice went for the kill and scored a quick touchdown to pull within two, 21–19. On the vital two-point conversion attempt, cornerback Michael Hawthorne stayed with his man and deflected the pass, preserving the win for the home team.

Brees finished 21 of 30 for 250 yards and two scores through the air while running for a third. It was the first of what would be twenty-four wins as a starting quarterback for the Old Gold and Black in the following three seasons, ultimately peaking in his senior season with a Big Ten title and a trip to the Rose Bowl.

OCTOBER 23, 1998

PURDUE 56, MINNESOTA 21—BREES REWRITES THE RECORD BOOKS

Purdue and Minnesota played some all-time great games throughout the course of more than a century as two founding members of the Big Ten. The 1998 edition in the series was anything but great—at least as far as Minnesota is concerned.

Purdue came into the contest fresh off a 31–30 loss at Notre Dame, dropping the Boilermakers to 2-2 on the year. The Gophers entered the game with a perfect 3-0 record but hadn't really been tested. They were about to get a test like few had ever seen.

The Gophers made the mistake of thinking that they could challenge Tiller's offense with man-to-man coverage in the secondary. It was a strategy that had the entire Purdue offense eager with anticipation as they prepared for the challenge. And it didn't take long to see how this script was going to play out.

In the first quarter, Brees completed 10 of 11 through the air for 201 yards and two scores. Brees added two more touchdowns in the second quarter, and Purdue ran its advantage to 35–7 at the half. He threw for two more scores in the third quarter before calling it a day. When all was said and done, Brees finished 31 of 36 through the air for 522 yards and six scores while sitting out the entire fourth quarter. He set the single-game records for passing yards, passing touchdowns, passing efficiency and total offense while having the third-best completion percentage in school history.

Brees wasn't the only Boilermaker to shine that day. Randall Lane, Gabe Cox and Cliff Jackson became the first trio of receivers to break the century mark in the same game. Only one of Purdue's eight scoring drives took more than five minutes off the game clock, while four of them lasted two minutes or less. The offense reached the end zone on eight of its first nine drives on the day and had twenty-four plays gain 10 yards or more on the afternoon. And in the best game of his college career, backup quarterback David Edgerton completed 4 of 7 for 82 yards as the Purdue passing game combined for more than 600 yards through the air.

The Boilermakers would go on to finish 9-4 and win their second-consecutive Alamo Bowl, taking down no. 4 Kansas State on a dramatic last-minute touchdown pass from Brees to Ike Jones.

SEPTEMBER 11, 1999

NO. 20 PURDUE 28, NO. 16 NOTRE DAME 23—"LET'S BLITZ 'EM" PAYS OFF FOR TILLER

The Joe Tiller era is historic for its offensive innovation, bringing the spread offense to the Big Ten and instituting the "Basketball on Grass" mentality. In the second game of the 1999 season, however, it was the decision made by the program's one-time defensive coordinator that made all the difference.

With sixteen seconds to go in the game, Notre Dame trailed by five and had driven down to the Purdue 1-yard line. On third-and-goal, defensive coordinator Brock Spack looked to his mentor for advice, and Tiller said three vital words: "Let's blitz 'em." Fighting Irish quarterback Jarious Jackson took the snap and began to roll to his left on a quarterback sweep. The Boilermakers rushed eight men forward. On the near side, cornerback Adrian Beasley set the edge, while defensive end Brian Dinkins got a free run thanks to the attention Notre Dame was giving to Akin Ayodele. On the far side, linebacker Mike Rose and cornerback Lamar Conard gave chase. They met at the quarterback, bringing down Jackson for a 9-yard loss. Amid the chaos of that play, Notre Dame realized that they were out of timeouts, and the clock expired before they could get another snap off.

The Boilermakers had rallied from a 16–7 deficit to snatch the victory away from the Irish. Drew Brees got the Boilers on the board with a 9-yard run late in the first quarter and then connected with Randall Lane on a 30-yard touchdown pass in the final minutes of the second to cut the halftime deficit to 16–14. The Boilermakers briefly took the lead midway through the third quarter as J. Crabtree took an option pitch around the left end for a 1-yard touchdown. On the two-point conversion, Brees rolled right and saw a clear path to the corner of the end zone. As he dove for the pylon, he was hit by a trio of Notre Dame defenders, helicoptered around a full 360 degrees and landed in the end zone for a 22–16 lead.

The Irish answered right back with a ten-play, 75-yard drive and retook the lead 23–22. A pair of fourth-quarter field goals by Travis Dorsch would prove to be the difference in the 28–23 final score. Drew Brees threw for 317 yards and a touchdown while also leading the team with 39 rushing yards, a touchdown and that iconic two-point conversion.

It was the eighth consecutive victory for the Boilermakers spanning back to the end of the 1998 season, and it thrilled the sellout crowd of more than sixty-nine thousand fans packed into the stands at Ross-Ade, the largest crowd to fill the stadium since 1981.

SEPTEMBER 25, 1999

PURDUE 31, NORTHWESTERN 23—99 YARDS FOR THE WIN!

By the time the Boilermakers opened the 1999 Big Ten season in Ross-Ade, the squad had run its winning streak to nine straight spanning two seasons. They would welcome a Northwestern program that had won a pair of Big Ten titles in the mid-'90s, but by the end of the decade the program had fallen back to earth. That is why the Wildcat team that came to Ross-Ade to face the thirteenth-ranked Boilermakers were four-touchdown underdogs. The game itself ended up being much better than Vegas could've imagined.

Purdue jumped out to an early 10–0 lead thanks to a 47-yard Travis Dorsch field goal and a 2-yard pass from Drew Brees to Vinny Sutherland. The Wildcats had cut the lead to 10–7 by intermission and then took a 14–10 lead on the opening drive of the second half. J. Crabtree broke free for a 47-yard score to push Purdue back in front, and the Wildcats immediately tied the game at 17 on a short field goal.

On the next Purdue drive, the Boilermakers set up a patented bubble screen to Vinny Sutherland. The problem was that Northwestern linebacker Kevin Bentley read it perfectly, stepped in front of Sutherland and sprinted 40 yards the other way for a pick-six. Purdue blocked the PAT, and the lead was 6. Brees bounced right back, however, engineering a scoring drive that covered 65 yards in less than two minutes, connecting with Tim Stratton for the touchdown as Purdue took a 24–23 lead.

Midway through the fourth quarter, a perfect Wildcat punt pinned the Boilermakers at their own 2-yard line. Clinging to a one-point lead, a two-point safety would've been devastating. That's nearly what happened as Montrell Lowe took a handoff on first down and was hit immediately, barely squirming forward out of the end zone for a loss of a yard. Lowe got nothing on second down, and on third-and-11, the Boilermakers were hoping for a first down. When Northwestern showed an aggressive look, Brees audibled to a shot play. At the snap, Sutherland took off. Brees dropped back, side-stepped a Wildcat defender and heaved a ball that traveled 55 yards in the air and landed perfectly in Sutherland's cradled arms at the opposite 45-yard line. By the time Vinny stopped running, he had covered 99 yards for the score, the longest play in school history.

The win ran the Boilermakers' win streak to double-digits, the longest since the program won eleven straight from 1928 to 1930. After the game, Brees was upset with his performance despite throwing for more than 400 yards, and Tiller was angry with his team's performance in general, which perfectly illustrated just how for the program had come in just a few short years.

OCTOBER 16, 1999

No. 20 PURDUE 52, No. 5 MICHIGAN STATE 28—TILLER DEMOLISHES SABAN'S SPARTANS

After running their winning streak to ten games, the Boilermakers' reward was back-to-back road trips to Ann Arbor and Columbus to play Top 20 opponents in front of more than ninety thousand people. After dropping both, Joe Tiller's crew returned home to face undefeated, fifth-ranked Michigan State. It was a daunting challenge to be sure and could have sent a once-promising season completely off the rails. The Boilermakers responded with possibly the best statistical game in program history.

The Spartans took the opening kick and drove 91 yards for a score. Less than five minutes into the game, the Homecoming crowd of more than sixty-eight thousand people had to be wondering what they were in for. By the end of the first quarter, they had their answer. Quarterback Drew Brees responded to MSU's touchdown drive with a quick strike, hitting Chris Daniels for a 51-yard touchdown on a drive that lasted exactly two minutes.

On the first play of the ensuing drive, MSU's star receiver Plaxico Burress fumbled, and twenty-seven seconds later, Brees hit Vinny Sutherland for a touchdown. Brees added a third touchdown pass later in the quarter, following an interception by Adrian Beasley, and the Boilermakers led 21–6 after one. In the first frame, Brees was 7 of 8 for 121 yards and three scores.

The second quarter saw Brees throw for two more scores, and at the half, Purdue led 35–14. Brees had amassed 344 yards through the air to go with five touchdowns, the only blemish being a pair of interceptions. The Spartans put together an early second-half touchdown drive and

Quarterback Drew Brees rewrote the record book, leaving Purdue as the career leader in attempts, completions, passing yards, completion percentage, touchdowns and total offense. *Purdue Athletics.*

then got their second pick-six of the afternoon to pull to within 35–28. Then the offense cranked it up again as Brees completed five passes in a row for 70 yards on the ensuing drive before finishing things off with a rushing touchdown. Purdue added 10 more points in the fourth quarter with a Travis Dorsch field goal and a strip-sack by Akin Ayodele that David Nugent recovered and took 12 yards for the final score of the day. The Boilermakers had taken down the mighty Spartans 52–28.

Brees finished the day forty for fifty-seven through the air for 509 yards and five scores while rushing for a sixth. His favorite target on the afternoon was senior receiver Chris Daniels, who set Big Ten records with twenty-one receptions and 301 yards with three scores. Amazingly, fourteen of Daniels's receptions were for first downs. But as great as the offensive numbers were, the Boilermaker defense was even better, surrendering just 44 yards on the ground while forcing six turnovers and recording five sacks.

The defensive performance was so great that defensive coordinator Brock Spack lost a bet with his team. He promised that he would shave his legendary mustache if the Boilers held Michigan State to fewer than 100 yards on the ground, forced three turnovers and won the game. In the celebration afterward, Spack stayed true to his word, letting Beasley and linebackers Mike Rose, Willie Fells and Jason Loerzel do the honors.

Nick Saban left Michigan State after the season and would go on to win a national title at LSU and six more at Alabama, forcing himself into the discussion of greatest college football coaches ever. But he never beat the great Joe Tiller.

2000s
RETURN TO GLORY

BREES, ORTON AND KERRIGAN

October 7, 2000

Purdue 32, No. 6 Michigan 31—The Run to the Roses Begins

Poised for special things heading into the 2000 season, the Boilermakers were reeling after the season's first five weeks, standing at 3-2 overall and 1-1 in the Big Ten. A road loss at Penn State knocked the squad out of the Top 25, and frustration began to boil over. In postgame comments to the media, quarterback Drew Brees directly called out the special teams after two botched punts led to a pair of short scoring drives for PSU and kicker Travis Dorsch missed a field goal in the fourth quarter that could have made the difference in the 22–20 final.

The Boilermakers returned home in desperate need of a win. They'd be taking on sixth-ranked Michigan. Things couldn't have started worse. The Wolverines scored a touchdown on their first drive and then held the Boilermakers out of the end zone, forcing a short Dorsch field goal after an 81-yard drive. Michigan took a 14–3 lead early in the second quarter and then intercepted a Brees pass in the end zone to kill another Purdue drive.

Michigan running back Anthony Thomas broke free for a 61-yard scoring run less than two minutes later, and the Wolverines were up 21–3. Brees connected with receiver Vinny Sutherland to temporarily stop the bleeding, but Michigan scored again in the closing seconds of the first half to go up

It took two tries, but junior kicker Travis Dorsch made good on the one that mattered to take down Michigan and save the season. *Purdue Athletics.*

28–10 at the break. The Wolverines drove 80 or more yards on all four first-half possessions, finding the end zone each time.

Purdue received the second-half kickoff, and Brees drove the team 75 yards on eleven plays, with Steve Ennis scoring from a yard out. A two-point try failed, leaving the score 28–16. The Boilermaker defense forced Michigan to punt for the first time all day, giving the ball back to the offense. This time, the Boilermakers went on a thirteen-play, 80-yard drive, with Montrell Lowe finishing it with a 16-yard scoring run. Brees completed 6 of 7 pass attempts on the drive for 44 yards and ran for another 17 yards. He also passed Mark Herrmann to become the program's all-time passing leader on the drive. But most importantly, the Boilermakers had pulled to within five, 28–23.

Michigan added a field goal early in the fourth, and the Boilermakers responded with another 80-yard drive, with Brees hitting receiver John Standeford for the final 10 yards. Another failed two-point try left the Wolverines still on top 31–29. The defense forced a three-and-out, getting the ball right back with just under five minutes remaining.

After driving into the red zone, Dorsch trotted out with just over two minutes remaining for the go-ahead field goal. But his 32-yard attempt faded wide left, and it looked to all sixty-eight thousand in attendance that the Boilermakers may lose a third game by less than 3 because of a late special teams mistake. The defense had other ideas.

On first down, Michigan ran Thomas up the middle for no gain. Timeout Purdue with 2:03 to play. On second down, the Wolverines tried an end-around with Ronald Bellamy, but defensive end Ike Moore blew it up, hitting Bellamy 3 yards deep in the backfield. Ralph Turner finished off the tackle for a 2-yard loss. Purdue used its final timeout, setting up third-and-long with 1:56 remaining.

Michigan elected to pass the ball and try to pick up the first down, but quarterback Drew Henson missed high, stopping the clock and forcing a punt. Sutherland got a 10-yard return after a great kick, setting the offense up at their 40-yard line with 1:41 remaining. On first down, after nothing was open downfield, Brees took off for an 11-yard gain and a first down. On the next play, Brees had to throw his pass away. He hit A.T. Simpson for an 8-yard gain on second down, bringing up a key third down with the clock ticking under a minute. Brees fired a 5-yard out to John Standeford for the first down. Even better, the true freshman had the poise to step out of bounds, stopping the clock. Sutherland stepped out of bounds after another 5-yard gain, and then Brees fired to Vinny in the middle of the field for a first down at the 21-yard line.

Michigan tried to bring fresh linemen on, but Brees noticed it and hurried the snap, picking up a free 5 yards, catching the Wolverines with thirteen men on the field. A first-down handoff to Lowe went for just a yard as Coach Joe Tiller decided that they were close enough for another field goal attempt.

With eight seconds to go, Dorsch lined up for redemption. This time, the kick hooked just inside the left upright, giving the Boilermakers the 32–31 win. Season saved.

The offense was great in the win, converting an astounding fourteen of eighteen third-down opportunities. Brees threw for 286 yards and ran for

80 more. Lowe gained 126 on the ground, while Sutherland caught eleven passes for 127 yards. Even more impressive was the second-half defensive effort, as they held Michigan to 79 yards and just three points in the final two quarters. It was a great team win. And the true magic of the 2000 season was only just beginning.

October 28, 2000

No. 16 Purdue 31, No. 12 Ohio State 27—"Holy Toledo!"

The magical month of October 2000 included the miracle over Michigan and road wins at no. 17 Northwestern and Wisconsin, where Ashante Woodyard returned a blocked field goal for a touchdown in overtime for the win. That win left Purdue at 6-2, 4-1 in Big Ten play, and still in the thick of the conference title picture. The last Saturday of the month brought no. 12 Ohio State to town.

The Buckeyes came into the game at 6-1 overall, 3-1 in the Big Ten, having spent the entire season ranked. After a scoreless first quarter, the Buckeyes got on the board first with a field goal after intercepting quarterback Drew Brees near midfield. A rushing touchdown by Steve Ennis put the Boilermakers up 7–3 at the half in what was a shockingly low score considering the explosive potential of both offenses.

The teams traded field goals to start the third quarter, and then the Buckeyes went on top, 13–10, with a 62-yard touchdown drive. The Buckeyes then forced a three-and-out, and future first-round NFL draft pick Nate Clements returned the punt 83 yards to pay dirt, putting OSU up 20–10 after three quarters. Brees and company would have fifteen minutes to save the season—again.

Brees connected with receiver John Standeford on third-and-goal early in the fourth quarter to make it 20–17 OSU. After the defense forced a quick punt, the Purdue offense went back to work, driving 90 yards on thirteen plays, with Brees hitting receiver Vinny Sutherland for the final 19, giving the home team the 24–20 lead with less than six minutes to go. On the scoring play, another third-and-long situation, Drew hit Vinny on an underneath pattern, hoping to pick up the first down. Sutherland caught the ball, and as he turned up field, he was 3 yards short of the marker. He slammed on the breaks to let a defender go flying by and then immediately hit the gas, sprinting past three Buckeye defenders before diving for the pylon.

The Buckeyes caught a massive break on first down of their next drive when quarterback Steve Bellisari appeared to have fumbled when defensive end Akin Ayodele sacked him, but it was ruled down. The Boilermakers recovered the would-be fumble inside the 20-yard line, but it didn't matter. Incomplete passes on the next two plays forced a punt. A penalty negated a great return by Sutherland, putting the Boilermakers in poor field position. Still, less than five minutes remained. The Boilermakers had a four-point lead and the ball. Then disaster struck.

Montrell Lowe lost 2 yards on first down, and Brees picked up 6 on second down. On third down, Brees dropped back to pass and faced immediate pressure. He lost his footing as he tried to throw the ball away and left it short of the sideline, with Buckeye safety Mike Doss the only player within 5 yards of the ball. Doss returned Brees's fourth interception of the day to the 2-yard line before being knocked out of bounds by the quarterback. The Buckeyes took nearly a minute off the clock before retaking the lead, 27–24.

On the Purdue sideline, defensive end Ike Moore came up to Brees to offer vital words of encouragement. "Hey, what's your mom always tell you?

"WIDE OPEN…GOT HIM! Touchdown Purdue! Seth Morales…Holy Toledo!" Brent Musberger, October 28, 2000. *Purdue Athletics.*

If you break it, then go fix it," Moore told his fellow senior in a moment briefly caught on ABC's broadcast. By the end of the exchange, both men were smiling.

Senior Chris Clopton jump-started the final drive with a 31-yard kick return, giving Purdue decent field position with just over two minutes remaining. After a deflected pass on first down, it was second-and-10 with 2:03 remaining. The offense set up with four wide receivers, Lowe standing next to Brees in the backfield. At the snap, Drew looked first to Standeford, wide left—covered. Next was Sutherland in the slot on the left—covered. A.T. Simpson was in the slot on the right, and that was Drew's third progression. Doss had jumped that route, anticipating a throw across the middle. That left the fourth option, Seth Morales, split far right— wide open.

"Offensive line continues to do a great jo—Wide Open…Got Him," screamed ABC announcer Brent Musberger. "Touchdown Purdue! Seth Morales! Holy Toledo!"

Morales dropped to a knee as he came to a stop in the end zone and pointed a single finger skyward. At that exact moment, 75 yards away, Brees had dropped to a knee as well, his left hand at his forehand in disbelief. He was quickly embraced by his offensive line, while Morales was mobbed by his fellow receivers. As Brees got to the sideline, waiting there to shake his hand was none other than Ike Moore. Drew had fixed it.

On the day, Brees was finished with 455 yards and three scores. More importantly, with two games to go, the path to Pasadena was clearly laid out for the Boilermakers.

November 18, 2000

No. 17 Purdue 41, Indiana 13—A Three-Hour Celebration

The 2000 Big Ten Football season was as wide open as any in history. When the Boilermakers beat Ohio State, they improved to 5-1 in the conference with two games remaining. The following week, Michigan and Northwestern played an all-time classic in Evanston, with the Wildcats winning 54–51 to improve to 5-1 also. However, a head-to-head loss to Purdue left the Boilermakers with the inside track to the Rose Bowl if they could just take care of Michigan State and Indiana, two teams tied for last place in the league standings. Well, it's never as easy as it sounds.

Left: Drew Brees takes a moment on the sideline to celebrate the program's second-ever trip to Pasadena. *Purdue Athletics.*

Right: Coach Joe Tiller and his prized pupil, Drew Brees, take a moment to enjoy the win over IU, clinching the Big Ten title and a trip to the Rose Bowl. *Purdue Athletics.*

An uninspired performance in East Lansing led to a 30–10 loss to the Spartans, and the Boilermakers were in danger of falling behind Northwestern. They caught a break, however, when the Wildcats were also upset in the season's penultimate game, falling to Iowa at home. Michigan had held serve to make it a three-way tie at the top, but the Boilermakers still held wins over both the Wolverines and the Wildcats, so they knew that if they beat Indiana, it was off to Pasadena.

There was plenty of motivation as kickoff approached. Not only was a Big Ten title on the line, but it was also Senior Day for Drew Brees, Matt Light, Vinny Sutherland, Tim Stratton and several other players who had been vital to the resurrection of Purdue Football. It was also a battle for the Bucket, which no one on the team had ever lost. Much to the sellout crowd's delight, in a season that had plenty of drama, the final game of the 2000 season was more like a coronation.

Stratton and Montrell Lowe scored in the first quarter, and Brees added a 2-yard rushing touchdown in the second to give Purdue a 20–7 lead at the half. Lowe scored twice more in the third quarter to put the home team up

34–7 with 15 minutes remaining. The Hoosiers scored on the first play of the fourth quarter before Lowe added his fourth and final touchdown of the day to close out the 41–13 win. Lowe had his finest day as a Boilermaker, going for 208 yards on the ground to go with his four scores.

As fans swarmed onto the field for the third time of the season, red roses were everywhere—pictures on the video board, in Drew Brees's mouth and painted on the bare chests of several brave souls in the student section on this chilly November evening. A bouquet was handed to Coach Joe Tiller for a photo opportunity, and the grin on his face would've been enough to illuminate the stadium.

After a season full of miracles, the Boilermakers were Big Ten champions. And for the first time since 1967, they were headed back to the Rose Bowl.

September 22, 2001

Purdue 33, Akron 14—"I Am an American"

"I am an American. That's how most of us put it, just matter-of-factly…." So begins the traditional introduction to the national anthem at Ross-Ade Stadium as performed by the university's All-American Marching Band. It is a tradition that began in the 1960s, but perhaps its most important and poignant iteration was performed on September 22, 2001. Eleven days earlier, the United States had come under attack when terrorists hijacked four airplanes and crashed them into the World Trade Center, the Pentagon and a field in eastern Pennsylvania, less than two hundred miles from the U.S. Capitol.

Many things had come to a halt around the country in the days following the attacks on 9/11, including college sports. Purdue's home opener against Notre Dame that weekend was postponed until December, so when more than sixty-three thousand people showed up to Ross-Ade for the Akron game, it was the first time many had been in a large gathering since the attacks.

Security was heightened at the stadium. A no-fly zone over Ross-Ade meant that there would be no small planes carrying banners circling overhead. A general uneasiness accompanied many to their seats that day. And then the AAMB took the field, and Roy S. Johnson, the band's public address announcer, took center stage. After a moment of silence, Johnson began, "I am an America…."

Tears filled the eyes of many in attendance as they mouthed the words that had suddenly taken on a much deeper meaning. American flags popped

Any Purdue fan will tell you that there are few traditions better than the "I am an American!" tradition, which was never more important than on September 22, 2001. *Purdue Athletics.*

up sporadically around Ross-Ade Stadium all afternoon. The field itself was ringed in Stars and Stripes for the occasion.

The Boilermakers handled the Zips for a 33–14 win, with the defense leading the way, holding Akron to 266 yards of offense and forcing three turnovers. Running back Joey Harris ran for two touchdowns, and receiver John Standeford caught two scores from quarterback Brandon Hance as the Boilermakers improved to 2-0 on the year.

But more important than the home team winning the game was that the game happened at all. Sometimes sports are a silly sideshow, a distraction from a mundane day-to-day routine. But on this day, this event was vitally important because of its power to unite and heal. "So, whenever you speak them, speak them firmly, speak them proudly, speak them gratefully. I am an American."

November 9, 2002

Purdue 6, No. 3 Ohio State 10—Oh So Close

In the 2002 college football season, no one beat the Ohio State Buckeyes. Few teams came close, and none came closer than Coach Joe Tiller's Boilermakers. In the midst of a disappointing up-and-down season, the

Boilermakers came into the early November game with a 4-5 record, having lost three of their last four. The Buckeyes, meanwhile, were averaging more than thirty-three points per game, were outscoring opponents by nearly three touchdowns and had climbed into the AP Top 3.

The Boilermakers took a 3–0 lead in the first quarter on a 21-yard field goal by Berin Lacevic following a Niko Koutouvides interception. The Buckeyes pulled even with a field goal in the second quarter to make it 3–3 at the half. Lacevic hit another field goal in the fourth quarter to put the Boilermakers back up 6–3 with less than eight minutes to go.

The Buckeyes offense couldn't find a rhythm all game, averaging just 2.4 yards per carry on the ground. The Boilermakers forced a punt, giving the offense the ball back with the lead and under five minutes remaining, but the offense went nowhere, punting it right back. The Buckeyes got the ball back near midfield with just over three minutes to go.

On first down, Ralph Turner sacked OSU quarterback Craig Krenzel for a 4-yard loss. Second down brought an incomplete pass, setting up third-and-long with 2:26 to go. A third-down pass went for 12, and the Buckeyes faced a fourth-and-2 with the clock running. Krenzel took the snap, dropped back and then stepped up in the pocket and heaved toward the end zone, where receiver Michael Jenkins created just enough separation from Antwaun Rogers to make the catch for the touchdown with 1:36 remaining.

The Buckeyes would go on to beat Illinois and Michigan to earn a spot in the national title game, where they defeated Miami for the national title. The Boilermakers rallied to beat Michigan State and Indiana, clinching a sixth straight bowl game for Coach Tiller. In the Sun Bowl, they handled Washington to finish 7-6 on the year. And they came oh so close to dethroning the eventual champions.

SEPTEMBER 20, 2003

NO. 25 PURDUE 59, ARIZONA 7—*EVERYTHING* CLICKS AGAINST THE CATS

Expectations were high for the Boilermakers heading into the 2003 season. The squad ended the 2002 season on a three-game winning streak, including a win over Washington in the Sun Bowl. The only loss in the season's final month had come to national champion Ohio State. The Boilermakers returned eighteen starters, including junior quarterback

After several rough years, sellouts became a regular occurrence once more during the Tiller era, with capacity settling at 62,500 after the 2003 renovation. *Purdue Athletics.*

Kyle Orton and a veteran defense that was expected to be among the best the school had ever produced.

The Boilermakers began the season ranked sixteenth in the AP Poll and promptly lost to Bowling Green in the season opener. A week two trip to Wake Forest went better, with the Boilermakers taking out the twentieth-ranked Demon Deacons, 20–16, but things still hadn't clicked for the squad. That all changed when Arizona came to the newly renovated Ross-Ade.

More than fifty-two thousand fans had a perfect afternoon for watching football, a cloudless seventy-two-degree day. They saw the home team jump out to an early lead when Orton hit receiver Ray Williams for a 35-yard scoring pass on the game's first drive. Jerod Void added a 2-yard scoring run early in the second, and then Ben Jones hit a 27-yard field goal to put the Boilermakers up 17–0. Both of those scoring drives came after the defense forced and recovered Arizona fumbles.

The Boilermakers got the ball back with under a minute to go in the first half at their own 19-yard line. That's when Orton found a streaking John Standeford, and 81 yards later, the Boilermakers had a 24–0 lead at the break. The second half was more of the same, with Antwaun Rogers getting an interception on the first Wildcat possession and Void adding his second scoring run of the day two plays later. Orton threw his third touchdown of the day later in the third quarter, finding running back Brandon Jones for the 43-yard score. It was 38–0 Purdue before Arizona got its first, and only, score of the day.

In the fourth quarter, second-string quarterback Brandon Kirsch threw a touchdown to receiver Kyle Ingraham, and running back Jerome Brooks had a pair of rushing touchdowns. Offensively, the Boilermakers were very balanced, with 292 yards on the ground to go with 288 yards through the air. Orton finished 16 of 28 for 261 yards and three scores in less than three quarters of action. But the real stars of the day came on defense.

Landon Johnson finished with four tackles including a sack, two force fumbles including one recovery and an interception. The Boilermakers held Arizona to just 174 yards of total offense, including just 66 rushing yards, while forcing four turnovers and making the Wildcats punt eleven times. The season had definitely turned around for the Boilermakers, as they would go on to handle Notre Dame the following week and reel off six straight wins.

November 8, 2003

No. 16 Purdue 27, No. 10 Iowa 14—Defense, Running Game Handle Hawks

Head Coach Joe Tiller is a legend at Purdue for bringing "Basketball on Grass" to the Big Ten, slinging the ball all over the place in high-scoring affairs. The early November game against a Top 10–ranked Iowa Hawkeye team was the exact opposite of that.

It was Senior Day for a group of guys who had seen their first action during the 2000 Rose Bowl season, including Gilbert Gardner, Landon Johnson, Niko Koutouvides, Shaun Phillips, Stuart Schweigert, John Standeford and Craig Terrill. They would all have a say in the final outcome.

The game figured to be a defensive battle, with both teams featuring defenses ranked in the nation's Top 10. Sophomore running back Jerod Void got the Boilermakers on the board early with a 9-yard scoring run in the game's opening minutes. Kicker Ben Jones added a pair of field goals in the second quarter, including a 42-yarder as the first half expired, giving Purdue a 13–0 lead at the break.

The Boilermakers received the kick at the start of the third quarter, and Jerome Brooks kept the momentum going with a 47-yard return out to midfield. It took Orton all of three plays to cover the remaining 50 yard as he hit Anthony Chambers for a 45-yard touchdown pass on third down. Just over a minute into the second half, Purdue led 20–0. Void scored a second touchdown later in the third quarter to all but put the game away. The Hawkeyes scored the game's final two touchdowns to make it a respectable 27–14, but they never actually threatened a real comeback.

On the day, the Purdue ground game racked up 154 rushing yards, more than double what Iowa's vaunted defense had been surrendering on average for the year. Void led the way with 120 yards and two scores. Orton was an efficient 13 of 20 for 167 yards and a touchdown as the Purdue offense called more than twice as many run plays as pass plays for the day.

Defensively, the Boilermakers surrendered just 98 rushing yards and 301 yards of total offense on the day while accumulating eleven tackles for a loss. Purdue would fall out of a three-way tie for the Big Ten lead with an overtime loss at Ohio State the next week but rallied to beat IU on the season's final day to finish the regular season 9-3 and clinch a Capital One Bowl bid.

September 5, 2004

No. 25 Purdue 51, Syracuse 0—Opening Day Perfection

One thing everyone knew headed into the 2004 season was that the team would look very different, particularly on defense. Nine Boilermakers were drafted in April 2004, including seven defensive starters. Quarterback Kyle Orton was back for his senior year and would have weapons aplenty, but the Boilermakers knew that it could be a challenging start to the season.

In a first for Ross-Ade Stadium, the game with Syracuse was moved to Sunday afternoon and made into a national television spectacle on Labor Day weekend. The day got off to a slow start with a pair of Syracuse punts and a missed Purdue field goal. The rest of the first half made up for it.

Jerod Void scored on a 1-yard sweep to the left to put Purdue up with four minutes remaining in the first quarter. The defense forced another Syracuse punt, and Orton's offense took over on the Purdue 25-yard line. On first down, Orton took the shotgun snap and pump-faked a wide receiver screen before looking long. The Syracuse safety fell for it just enough, and Kyle hit receiver Brian Hare streaking down the sideline for a 75-yard score. For the Boilermakers, the race was on.

Taylor Stubblefield got in on the action in the second quarter with a 33-yard touchdown reception, and Purdue led 20–0 at the break. In the third quarter, Stubblefield went 67 yards on another one-play drive to make it 27–0. Brandon Jones then caught a 32-yard touchdown, and Ben Jones added a field goal to make it 37–0 after three. Early in the fourth quarter, Jerome Brooks scored on a 44-yard run, while freshman tight end Dustin Keller caught a 47-yard touchdown pass from Brandon Kirsch in his Boilermaker debut to cap off the scoring. It was the Lafayette native's first career catch.

Orton finished with 267 yards and four scores through the air. The Boilermakers ran for 237 yards and totaled 571 yards of offense on the day. The young defense, meanwhile, nearly stole the show, allowing Syracuse just 40 yards rushing on thirty-two attempts and giving up a total of 197 yards of offense on the day in the shutout. It was the perfect start to the season and would get even better when Purdue beat Ball State 59–7 six days later, with Orton completing 23 of 26 for 329 yards and five scores. They then defeated Illinois on the road, demolished Notre Dame in South Bend and won at Penn State for the first time ever to begin the season 5-0 for the first time since 1945.

NOVEMBER 13, 2004

PURDUE 24, OHIO STATE 17—KELLER FOR THE WIN, ORTON WITH THE SAVE

The Boilermakers followed up the 5-0 start to the 2004 season with a four-game skid. Things went bad with a late fumble in a marquee matchup with Wisconsin, got worse when a late field goal made the difference in a loss to Michigan and then came completely undone in close road losses at Northwestern and no. 20 Iowa. Once 5-0 and ranked no. 5 in the AP Poll, Purdue was now 5-4, with those four losses coming by a total of ten points.

Next up on the docket was Ohio State, which came in at 6-3 and on a three-game winning streak. One-time Heisman Trophy candidate Kyle Orton would be missing his second straight start with a hip injury, although he told Coach Joe Tiller during pregame warmups that he could play if needed. Sophomore Brandon Kirsch would get his second straight start.

The teams traded first quarter field goals, and then the Purdue offense came to life in the second quarter. Kirsch hit receiver Kyle Ingraham for a 22-yard score early in the quarter to go up 10–3. The two connected for a second score with less than two minutes remaining to stake the Boilermakers to a 17–3 lead at the break.

Buckeye receiver Santonio Holmes made it 17–10 midway through the third quarter as the Buckeyes began to fight back into the game. Halfway through the fourth, still clinging to a lead, Kirsch threw an interception on an underneath route, and the Buckeyes seemed on the verge of tying the game up. But four plays later, safety Bernard Pollard forced a Buckeye fumble at the 5-yard line, and cornerback Brian Hickman recovered the loose ball.

Sensing that his offense might need a spark, Tiller called on Orton to relieve Kirsch. The drive went nowhere, and the Boilermakers had to punt. The Buckeyes finally took advantage of good field position, going 44 yards on seven plays with future Heisman Trophy–winning quarterback Troy Smith scoring on a 5-yard run to tie the game at 17–17. Orton had less than four minutes to go win the game.

The senior signal caller took his team 80 yards on eight plays, completing all six passes he attempted for 51 yards. On the game's deciding play, he hit freshman tight end Dustin Keller in the left flat on a second-down pass play. Keller raced toward the end zone and dove for the pylon in front of unanimous All-America linebacker A.J. Hawk to put the Boilermakers up 24–17. Purdue linebacker Stanford Keglar intercepted a desperate Ohio State pass on the Buckeye's final drive to ice the game.

It was a great team win for the Boilermakers. Orton completed 7 of 8 for 54 yards and a score, while Kirsch went 22 of 34 for 210 yards and two touchdowns. The defense forced four Buckeye turnovers, including two in the red zone. And the kicking game was perfect, with kicker Ben Jones going three for three on PATs and hitting his only field goal attempt.

The win not only put the Boilermakers back on the right side of the ledger for the first time in a month, but it was also Tiller's 100th win as a head coach, clinching an eighth straight bowl trip for the Boilermakers with a game to go.

November 20, 2004

Purdue 63, Indiana 24—Record-Setting Day for Orton, Stubblefield

As bitter as the 2004 season had been for Purdue fans, the final Saturday of the year provided a sweet finish to the season. It was Senior Day for quarterback Kyle Orton and his favorite receiver, Taylor Stubblefield, as well as defensive back Antwuan Rogers and a half dozen other Boilermakers. And, of course, it was the Bucket game.

The Hoosiers came in having lost six of their last seven games after a promising start to the season. And on this day, hope would disappear quickly. Purdue forced a three-and-out to start the game, and Orton took over. It took him just over a minute to drive 86 yards, connecting with receiver Kyle Ingraham for a 52-yard score. IU then kicked a field goal to pull within 4. It was as close as they would get the rest of the day.

Orton hit Stubblefield for a 23-yard score, and Brandon Jones ran for a 4-yard touchdown to make it 21–3 as the first quarter came to a close. On that scoring drive, Stubblefield caught a 7-yard reception from Orton to become the all-time NCAA leader in receptions with 301 catches.

In the second quarter, Orton hit Dorien Bryant for a 21-yard score, connected with Stubblefield for a 17-yard TD and went back to Ingraham for a 26-yard touchdown as the Boilermakers led 42–10 at the half. Orton and Stubblefield hooked up for a third touchdown on the opening drive of the second half to make it 49–10. Bryant opened the fourth quarter with a 62-yard touchdown run on a reverse, and backup quarterback Brandon Kirsch connected with tight end Charles Davis on a 61-yard touchdown pass

He had to go low to get it, but Taylor Stubblefield secured his NCAA-record 301ˢᵗ catch in his final home game in 2004. *Purdue Athletics.*

to close out the Boilermaker scoring for the day. When the final whistle blew, the scoreboard read Purdue 63, Indiana 24.

Orton finished the day 33 of 54 for 522 yards, tying Drew Brees's single-game yardage record. Stubblefield led a stellar receiving corps with fourteen catches for 138 yards and three scores, while Ingraham caught eleven balls for 209 yards and a pair of touchdowns and Bryant finished with five catches for 131 yards and a score. Kirsch threw for 68 yards and a score as the Boilermakers racked up 763 yards of total offense on the day, shattering the program record by more than 70 yards.

Defensively, defensive end Rob Ninkovich had nine tackles, including four sacks, on the day. For the second straight year, winning the Old Oaken Bucket meant that the Boilermakers would hold all three trophy games, having defeated Notre Dame for the Shillelagh and taken down Illinois for the Purdue Cannon.

September 9, 2006

Purdue 38, Miami (OH) 31 OT—Sheets Something Special

The 2006 season found the Boilermakers in a strange position under Head Coach Joe Tiller. It was the first time since he arrived in 1997 that the team wasn't coming off a bowl appearance. Tiller had gone eight for eight until falling just short of the postseason in 2005.

Because of that, getting off to a good start in 2006 was vitally important. The season began with a convincing win over FCS opponent Indiana State. In week two, the Miami Red Hawks came to town. The Mid-American Conference team gave the Boilermakers all they could handle, answering every Purdue score with one of their own. When sophomore running back Kory Sheets put the home team up with his third rushing touchdown of the day on the first play of the fourth quarter, Miami needed less than five minutes to tie the game at 24.

Sophomore quarterback Curtis Painter hit classmate Greg Orton on a one-play, 43-yard scoring drive to give the Boilers a 31–24 lead. Miami scored on its next drive, and the game was again deadlocked at 31. Purdue's offense had a chance to take a late lead, but Painter threw an interception with less than two minutes to go; the visitors seemed poised to take their first lead of the day when it mattered most. As the Red Hawks lined up for a game-winning field goal on the final play of the day, defensive end Anthony

Spencer had one of the greatest plays of his career. The senior out of Fort Wayne burst through the line and blocked the field goal to force overtime.

In overtime, Sheets ran for his fourth touchdown of the day, and the defense held Miami out of the end zone to preserve the win. Sheets finished with just 60 rushing yards, but his four scores tied for the second most in a single game in program history.

SEPTEMBER 23, 2006

PURDUE 27, MINNESOTA 21—OFFENSE, DEFENSE AND SPECIAL TEAMS

After failing to go to a bowl game for the first time in his Purdue tenure following the 2005 season, Coach Joe Tiller had the team firing on all cylinders to begin the 2006 season. Three straight home wins opened the season, and although the team wasn't always perfect, the record was. Next up was the Big Ten opener against Minnesota.

Minnesota took the opening kickoff and drove 83 yards on fifteen plays, using nearly half of the first quarter and finishing in the end zone. The Boilermakers responded with a Chris Summers field goal, and the score was 7–3 after one.

The Gophers were looking to extend their lead late in the second quarter when Purdue defensive tackle Alex Magee blocked a 51-yard field goal attempt. Quarterback Curtis Painter covered 42 yards in three plays, hitting receiver Dorien Bryant for a 27-yard score to put the home team up 10–7 at the half.

Purdue added to that lead on the opening possession of the second half when running back Jaycen Taylor scored on a 14-yard run. The Gophers saw their next drive end in disaster when defensive end Anthony Spencer sacked quarterback Bryan Cupito, forcing and recovering a Minnesota fumble. The offense took over at the Minnesota 38-yard line but had to settle for a field goal to make it 20–7. The Gophers scored on the final play of the third quarter to make it 20–14 with one quarter to go.

The Boilermakers then put together a nine-play, 93-yard scoring drive, with Painter connecting with Taylor for the 18-yard score to put the home team up 27–14. The Gophers pulled within 6 after converting two fourth-down plays on their final scoring drive, making it 27–21, but Purdue was able to run out the clock.

Painter finished 18 of 27 for 243 yards through the air, while Taylor led the ground game with 90 yards on just eleven carries to go with his first two career touchdowns as a Boilermaker. Justin Scott and Cliff Avril joined Spencer as the defensive leaders, notching ten tackles a piece. Spencer had two sacks, including the forced fumble and recovery, in one of his best games as a Boilermaker.

September 29, 2007

Purdue 33, Notre Dame 19—Strong Start, Great Finish

The 2007 season got off to a scorching-hot start for the Boilermakers, but it wasn't just the 4-0 record. Purdue scored fifty-two points in each of its first two games. Then Purdue put forty-five on the board in wins over Central Michigan and Minnesota, winning each game by at least two touchdowns. Next, they would welcome Notre Dame to town.

The Irish were going in the opposite direction under third-year head coach Charlie Weis. Notre Dame was 0-4, losing consecutive games to Penn State, Michigan and Michigan State. The sixty-five thousand Purdue fans in attendance were hoping to keep the Big Ten domination rolling.

After a field goal to open the game, the defense forced a quick three-and-out, and the Boilermakers went back to work. Quarterback Curtis Painter drove the team 80 yards on eight plays, with running back Kory Sheets crashing into the end zone from a yard out to make the score 10–0.

Cornerback Terrell Vinson intercepted a Jimmy Clausen pass early in the second quarter, and it turned into another short Chris Summers field goal. The defense forced another Notre Dame punt that Painter turned into points, connecting with receiver Dorien Bryant for an 11-yard score and a 20–0 lead. On Notre Dame's next play from scrimmage, linebacker Anthony Heygood forced a fumble on a screen pass, and defensive tackle Jeff Benjamin recovered at the Notre Dame 14-yard line. Summers converted another short field goal, and the lead was 23–0.

Defensive tackle Alex Magee blocked a field goal late in the half, and the Boilers led 23–0 at the break. Notre Dame finally scored midway through the third quarter, but a failed PAT left it 23–6. Summers added a career-best fourth field goal, making it 26–6 at the end of three.

The Irish scored early in the fourth quarter, with backup quarterback Evan Sharpley coming off the bench to lead the scoring drive. After forcing a quick punt, Sharpley led another scoring drive, hooking up with receiver Golden Tate making a diving catch for the score; it was now 26–19.

On their next possession, the Boilermaker offense kicked back into gear, with Painter hitting tight end Dustin Keller on a spectacular score, the Lafayette native twisting in midair to reach the ball across the goal line.

For the day, Sheets led the way for Purdue on the ground with 141 rushing yards on twenty-seven carries, while Painter finished with 252 passing yards and two scores. Defensively, the Boilermakers held Notre Dame to 49 yards rushing on twenty-six carries while forcing three turnovers and blocking a field goal. It was Coach Joe Tiller's fifth and final win over Notre Dame. Only Jack Mollenkopf had more success for the Boilermakers against the Irish.

September 20, 2008

Purdue 32, Central Michigan 25—All-Time Winner

The entire 2008 Purdue Football season took on a different meaning on January 11 when it was formally announced that the upcoming season would be Head Coach Joe Tiller's final season on the sidelines. Tiller stood one win shy of Jack Mollenkopf on the program's all-time wins list.

In week one, Tiller drew even with Mollenkopf with a win over Northern Colorado. A double-overtime loss to no. 16 Oregon in week two left the Boilermakers at 1-1 and Tiller still looking for the record breaker, although he downplayed its importance whenever he could.

Week three would be a familiar foe as Central Michigan came to Ross-Ade for the third matchup between the two programs in just over a calendar year. The Boilermakers had beaten the Chippewas in the regular season in 2007 and then again in a classic Motor City Bowl to conclude the 2007 season.

In the first quarter, kicker Chris Summers booted a field goal to put the home team up 3–0, but CMU responded with a touchdown. The second quarter was a mirror image of the first with the Chippewas hitting a field goal while Kory Sheets ran for a score, making it 10–10 at the half.

The only scoring in the third quarter came courtesy of the defense. Defensive tackle Mike Neal hit CMU quarterback Dan LeFevour as he released a third-down pass, and safety Frank Duong plucked the ball out of the air, racing 58 yards the other way for a pick-six and a 17–10 lead.

CMU tied it early in the fourth quarter, but quarterback Curtis Painter hit receiver Desmond Tardy for a short touchdown to put the home team back on top, 24–17.

The defense forced a turnover on downs, and the offense had a lead and the ball with four minutes to go. But on a third-and-1, Painter dropped the snap, scooped up the ball and dove for what appeared to be a key first down. But two CMU defenders hit him as he dove, dislodging the ball again and recovering the fumble.

The Chippewas drove 53 yards for a score, and with just over a minute remaining, Head Coach Butch Jones elected to go for the two-point conversion for the win. LeFevour hit sophomore receiver Antonio Brown to give the Chips a 25–24 lead.

Tardy took the ensuing kickoff out to the 39-yard line, and an extra 15 yards were tacked on at the end thanks to CMU facemask penalty. Kory Sheets would do the rest. On first down from the CMU 46-yard line, Painter lined up in shotgun formation, Sheets to his left. A pre-snap read led him to shift Sheets to the right side of the backfield. At the snap, Painter handed to Sheets. A jab step by the running back created enough time for a hole to develop, and he burst through the center of the line, past a diving linebacker.

A postgame ceremony celebrated Joe Tiller's eighty-fifth win. Quarterback Curtis Painter gives Arnette Tiller a hug while defensive tackle Ryan Baker and Athletics Director Morgan Burke look on. *Purdue Athletics.*

Ten yards downfield, with a safety stepping up to make the tackle, Sheets made a move that nearly defied physics. After breaking down almost to a complete stop, he feigned to the right and then exploded to the left—46 yards, untouched, and the Boilermakers were on top for good. Painter hit Orton for a two-point conversion, making it a 32–25 final. With the scoring run, Sheets became Purdue's all-time leader in touchdowns with forty-three. He wasn't the only one celebrating after the game.

After spending the previous weeks and months downplaying the significance of the wins record, Tiller walked into his postgame press conference puffing on a cigar, which defensive tackle Ryan Baker helped him light. "It feels damn good," Tiller said. "I've been very fortunate over the course of my career. I've been around a bunch of good assistants and players who played hard. When everyone's pulling on the oars together, good things happen."

November 1, 2008

Purdue 48, Michigan 42—Hook-and-Lateral for the Ages

After becoming the program's all-time winningest coach, things took a turn for Joe Tiller's team. Injuries began to pile up and so did the losses, leading to a five-game skid. Then Michigan came to town.

The Wolverines, under first-year head coach Rich Rodriguez, were mired in their worst season in four decades. But with football, lower stakes don't equate to a boring game. And this matchup would end up being anything but boring.

Michigan jumped out to a 14–0 lead thanks to a Purdue fumble and a 73-yard punt return for a score. The Boilermakers had drawn even by the end of the first quarter courtesy of a short scoring runs by running back Kory Sheets and quarterback Justin Siller.

Siller was getting his first career start because of injuries to starter Curtis Painter and backup Joey Elliott. The Wolverines jumped back on top with two quick scoring drives, but Sheets scored again with less than a minute to go to make it 28–21 at the half. Then Siller opened the second half with a 7-yard scoring pass to Sheets, and the game was tied.

Sheets scored his fourth touchdown of the day late in the third quarter, and the Boilermakers took their first lead, 35–28. Michigan used a long kickoff return and a short field to tie the game at 35–35 early in the fourth.

With ten minutes to go, Purdue's next drive went nowhere, bringing up fourth-and-8 from their own 32-yard line. Coach Tiller dialed up his first deception play of the afternoon, and it couldn't have been more perfect.

Linebacker Anthony Heygood was playing the fullback position in the punt formation, about 5 yards behind the long-snapper. Heygood, who began his Purdue career as a running back, took a direct snap and followed a great lead block by fellow linebacker Joe Holland. Once Heygood got past the initial wall of Maize and Blue defenders, there was nothing but green in front of him. He was finally tackled 61 yards later, inside the Michigan 10-yard line. Three plays later, Siller hit receiver Greg Orton for a touchdown and a 42–35 lead.

The Wolverines answered with a fourteen-play, 68-yard drive that lasted almost six minutes and ended with a touchdown, tying the game at 42–42. Siller and the Boilermakers would have just over a minute to answer. On first down, he hit receiver Keith Smith for 18 yards. On the next play, Siller hit receiver Desmond Tardy for a 20-yard gain into Michigan territory. Siller ran a quarterback draw for 3 yards and then called a timeout with thirty-three seconds to go. During that timeout, Tiller called his second deception play, and it became legendary.

With the Michigan secondary in an aggressive press coverage, Siller took the snap and almost immediately hit Orton on a 7-yard curl route. Just as his defender was closing to make a tackle, Orton tossed the ball to Tardy, who was sprinting across the field behind him. In addition to making a good catch and lateral, Orton also picked Tardy's defender, springing his teammate loose; 32 yards later, the Boilermakers retook the lead in one of the most spectacular plays Ross-Ade Stadium had ever seen.

Fittingly, the name of that triumphant play in the Boilermaker game plan was simply "Tiller."

November 22, 2008

Purdue 62, Indiana 10—One More for the Road

It's no stretch to say that Coach Joe Tiller's final season leading the Boilermakers didn't go as planned. Injuries led to a constantly revolving cast of offensive lineman and three different starting quarterbacks. A scheduling gauntlet that saw the Boilermakers play at Notre Dame, at no. 6 Penn State and at no. 12 Ohio State in consecutive weeks also didn't make things easy.

Coach Joe Tiller hoists the Old Oaken Bucket one final time, celebrating his eighty-seventh and final win at Purdue. *Purdue Athletics.*

So as the team headed to the Bucket game on the season's final week, there was only a trophy at stake. And pride. And one more chance to add to the legacy of a legend.

More than sixty-three thousand people turned out for Tiller's final game, and they got their money's worth. The old gunslinger decided to go out blazing, electing to begin the game in a two-minute, hurry-up offense mode. The game's first drive took just a little over two minutes to reach the end zone. The second drive took one play, with quarterback Curtis Painter hitting receiver Aaron Valentin for a 79-yard touchdown for a 14–0 lead. Painter added a third touchdown pass, and kicker Carson Wiggs connected on a short field goal. By the time the first quarter blitz was over, the home team was up 24–0. They weren't close to being done.

A pair of touchdown runs by Kory Sheets and another Wiggs field goal made it 41–3 at the half. Purdue had scored on all eight first-half possessions, while the defense forced three first-half turnovers. Painter threw for two more scores in the second half, hitting classmate Greg Orton in the third quarter and sophomore Keith Smith for another. Sheets also added a second-half score as the Boilermakers closed out the Bucket victory 62–10. There was a great moment at the beginning of the fourth quarter when Tiller's wife, Arnette, and their family led the stadium tradition of "Shout!"

Statistically, there were a lot of Boilermakers who stood out. Painter finished with 448 yards and five touchdowns through the air, while Sheets had three rushing scores to run his program record to fifty-four career touchdowns. Defensively, Purdue held IU to just 214 total yards while forcing three turnovers and four punts.

After the final whistle, a ceremony was held on the field in Ross-Ade Stadium with senior defensive tackle Ryan Baker introducing his coach. Tiller spoke of retirement and what Purdue meant to him, choking back tears when talking about his players through the years. "They say when you leave someplace, it's not what you take with you but what you leave behind," Tiller said. "Hopefully we left some great memories. I know we've left some great young men."

Tiller then hoisted the Old Oaken Bucket a final time and led the All-American Marching Band in a rendition of "Hail Purdue!," a tradition he vowed to start after every win a dozen years earlier. But no rendition was as bittersweet as the one that followed his eighty-seventh and final victory with the Boilermakers.

OCTOBER 17, 2009

PURDUE 26, NO. 7 OHIO STATE 18—KERRIGAN, WIGGS UPSET BUCKEYES

The post-Tiller era did not begin as planned for Purdue Football. After a season-opening win over Toledo, new head coach Danny Hope's teams had a string of heartbreaking losses. They fell by two on the road at Oregon and then returned home and lost by a touchdown to Northern Illinois. That was followed by a 24–21 loss to Notre Dame after the Irish found the end zone with twenty-four seconds left on the clock, a 6-point loss against Northwestern and a 15-point defeat at Minnesota.

The Boilermakers were 1-5 with the toughest game on the schedule next up as no. 7 Ohio State came to Ross-Ade Stadium. The Buckeyes came in having won sixteen straight conference games and were looking for one more to tie the Big Ten record.

Inspiration came in many forms that day. There was pride and the chance to turn the season around. There was the hope that correcting small things could lead to big results, often the case when a team is losing close games to good teams. And there was a text message late in the week from a former quarterback to the current starter.

"Go out and shock the world and have fun. I'll be watching," read the text from Drew Brees to Joey Elliott on Friday afternoon. That was the plan, and they wasted no time in getting into it.

Ohio State received the opening kick, and on the second play from scrimmage, defensive end Ryan Kerrigan sacked OSU quarterback Terrell Pryor, forcing a fumble that teammate Mike Neal recovered. Kicker Carson Wiggs turned that into 3 points, and the Boilermakers were on the board early. Pryor ran for a score on the Buckeyes' next drive to make it 7–3 Ohio State, and that's where the score stayed for the remainder of the quarter.

Midway through the second quarter, defensive back Adam Wolf recovered a muffed punt, and Wiggs again converted it into a short field goal to cut the lead to one, 7–6. The Buckeyes looked to extend their lead late in the first half with a drive that started at the Purdue 30-yard line after a bad punt

Defensive end Ryan Kerrigan dominated Ohio State with nine tackles, three sacks, two forced fumbles and a fumble recovery in the upset win. *Purdue Athletics.*

and quickly reached the red zone. Then Kerrigan struck again. On second down, the junior from Muncie whom his teammates had taken to calling "Superman" burst through the line and was in Pryor's face immediately. He drove Pryor backward 10 yards, stripping the ball along the way and then recovering the fumble. Wiggs kicked a 55-yard field goal as the first half expired to give the home team a 9–7 lead at the break.

The Boilermakers extended their lead when Elliott drove the team down the field on the opening drive of the third quarter, finding Aaron Valentin for a 15-yard touchdown. Later in the third, cornerback Brandon King intercepted Pryor for the second time, and Elliott hit Valentin for a 23-yard score; the home team went up 23–7. The teams traded field goals in the fourth quarter to make it 26–10. The Buckeyes reached the end zone with seven minutes to go, but it was too little, too late. The fans rushed the field to celebrate the team's first win over a ranked opponent since 2003, when they took down no. 10 Iowa.

The offense did enough, with Elliott finishing 31 of 50 for 280 yards and a pair of touchdowns. Receiver Keith Smith had twelve receptions for 125 yards, his fourth consecutive game with more than 100 yards receiving, while Valentin caught ten passes for 97 yards and both scores. The defense came up with a huge effort, holding the Buckeyes to 66 rushing yards, more than 110 yards below their season average, and just 287 yards of total offense while forcing five turnovers.

Superman finished with nine tackles, including four tackles for a loss, three sacks, two forced fumbles and a fumble recovery. His effort earned him the Walter Camp Foundation National Defensive Player of the Week honors, while he and Wiggs earned Big Ten Player of the Week awards.

The Boilermakers won four of their final six games, including a Bucket win, to finish 5-7.

2010s

CREATING LEGENDS

BROHM, MOORE AND TYLER TRENT

November 24, 2012

Purdue 56, Indiana 35—Out with a Bang

In what ended up being the final game of a four-year coaching tenure where seemingly every break went against Coach Danny Hope's team, everything went right in the 2012 battle for the Bucket. Although the twenty-one-point margin of victory suggests domination by the home team, it was anything but, as the Hoosiers scored first and held a 21–14 lead at the halfway point.

Behind senior quarterback Robert Marve, who was playing the game with a torn ACL in his left knee, the Boilermakers tied the game up with a touchdown on their first possession of the second half. Marve set the tone with a 31-yard scramble for a key first down and then hit receiver O.J. Ross for a touchdown. Second-string quarterback Rob Henry scored on a short run on Purdue's next possession and then Henry hit receiver Gary Bush for a touchdown to put the home team ahead 35–21 late in the third.

The Hoosiers scored in the closing minutes of the third quarter and then again early in the fourth to make it 35–35 with just over 12 minutes to play. On the ensuing kickoff, Raheem Mostert saw the ball bounce through his hands and off his chest while standing two yards deep in the end zone. The ball caromed out to the 1-yard line, where Mostert jumped on it. Disaster was narrowly averted, but now the Boilermakers took possession 99 yards from pay dirt. It would take Marve just four plays to cover that ground.

First down saw a 12-yard completion to fullback Brandon Cottom. Play two was a sweep right by Akeem Shavers that went nowhere. Play three was a 14-yard pass to Antavian Edison. Play four showed a heavy backfield formation with three running backs behind Marve. On the snap, the quarterback rolled right along with two of the backs. Shavers, the third back, sprinted to the left flat along with three linemen as Marve launched a perfect screen pass to the area. Shavers had 50 yards of wide-open space before two Hoosiers finally caught up to him, but he juked past one and stiff-armed the second, trotting into the end zone for a 73-yard score.

On Indiana's next possession, safety Max Charlot got an interception. Five plays later, Marve and Shavers hooked up again to go up 49–35. Indiana's next possession ended with an interception as well, with Antoine Lewis doing the honors. Shavers scored on a short run to make it 56–35 in favor of the good guys. In less than four and a half minutes of game time, the Boilermakers had scored 21 points, gained 145 yards and created two turnovers to retain the Bucket.

For the day, Marve finished with 348 yards and four touchdowns, while Shavers finished with 225 yards of total offense and three fourth-quarter touchdowns. The defense surrendered more than 500 yards but created four crucial second-half turnovers, each of which was converted into a touchdown by the offense.

The win made Purdue bowl eligible for the second consecutive year under Hope, although he would not be around to coach in that postseason game. Less than forty-eight hours after his team triumphantly carried him off the field, Hope was relieved of his coaching duties.

OCTOBER 31, 2015

PURDUE 55, NEBRASKA 45—TRACK MEET BREAKS OUT

Not every football game is destined to be a great contest between two elite teams with high stakes. The 2015 Nebraska-Purdue matchup certainly wasn't that. Nebraska was 3-5 on the year, 1-3 in conference play. The Boilermakers were worse, coming in at 1-6, 0-3 in league play. No, this wasn't going to be a great game with wide-ranging ramifications. But it sure was entertaining.

A back-and-forth affair saw Nebraska take a 3–0 lead before redshirt freshman quarterback David Blough scored on a 56-yard run to put Purdue up 7–3. Blough connected with receiver Danny Anthrop early in the second quarter for a 3-yard score, and then Domo Young scored on a short run to make it 21–9 at the half.

Nebraska opened the second half with a touchdown drive before Blough hooked up with tight end Jordan Jurasevich from 5 yards out to make it 28–16. After Nebraska's next drive ended in a punt, Blough hit receiver DeAngelo Yancey for an 83-yard scoring toss to make it 35–16. Cornerback Anthony Brown got his third interception of the day on Nebraska's next possession, and Blough hit Yancey for a second touchdown to put the home team up 42–16 after three quarters.

Two quick Nebraska touchdowns opened the fourth quarter, making it 42–31, and then cornerback Frankie Williams caught a tipped pass for an interception, setting up a short touchdown run by Markell Jones to make it 49–31 with less than six minutes remaining. It felt like a safe lead.

Nebraska scored quickly again to pull make it a two-score game. A failed onside kick attempt gave Purdue the ball in good field position, and Jones scored again with just over a minute remaining. The Huskers had one more desperate touchdown left in them, but when the final whistle blew, the home team stood victorious, 55–45. Blough finished with 274 yards and four scores through the air while rushing for 82 yards and a fifth. The defense forced five turnovers on the day, including Brown's three interceptions.

The two teams combined for one hundred points and 941 yards of total offense. Together, they converted fifteen of twenty-nine third-down attempts and two of three fourth-down conversions while going a perfect twelve for twelve on trips inside the red zone. The win wasn't pretty. But it sure was fun.

September 8, 2017

Purdue 44, Ohio 21—Impressive Debut Under the Lights

In his first game as head coach at Purdue, Jeff Brohm had the unenviable task of playing his alma mater, being led by reigning Heisman Trophy winner Lamar Jackson at quarterback—and at a neutral site no less. The Boilermakers came up just short on opening night, falling to no. 16 Louisville at Lucas Oil Stadium by a 35–28 score. Purdue then had to return home to play Ohio on a short week, but it was a game that was highly anticipated by the fan base. It would be a Friday night kickoff, in prime time, under the brand-new permanent lights at Ross-Ade Stadium.

The stadium had never had permanent light fixtures, bringing in temporary solutions whenever necessary. But it was the dawn of a new era, under a new leader. The largest crowd in nearly two seasons showed up and was treated to the home team jumping out to an early lead. A field goal by Spencer Evans and a touchdown pass from Elijah Sindelar to Brycen Hopkins put Purdue up 10–0 in the first.

Tario Fuller scored on a 1-yard run in the second, capping a nine-play, 97-yard drive to put Purdue up 17–7. A quick three-and-out gave the home team the ball back almost immediately, and the forty-six thousand in attendance got a glimpse of what the Brohm Squad was all about. From the pistol formation, quarterback David Blough took the first down snap and handed to running back D.J. Knox. Knox appeared to be bouncing the run outside to the right and then tossed the ball to slot receiver Jackson Anthrop, who had sprinted toward the backfield in a reverse run action. But Anthrop took the ball and immediately tossed it back to Blough, who looked downfield and saw tight end Cole Herdman standing all alone. One play, 62 yards, and the Boilermakers led 24–7.

Defensive end Austin Larkin forced a fumble that linebacker Danny Ezechukwu recovered on Ohio's next possession, and Evans turned it into another field goal with just under a minute to go in the first half. An incomplete pass on first down and a short run on second down led to a Purdue timeout with forty seconds to go. They wanted the ball back. On the next play, they got it, as Ohio ran a short swing pass to the running back and a big hit by linebacker Markus Bailey knocked the ball loose. Defensive tackle Gelen Robinson was there to scoop it up to give the offense one more possession. Blough would need just one play.

After a play-action fake to Knox, Blough dropped back and surveyed the defensive backfield. He found receiver Anthony Mahoungou all alone in the middle of the field and drilled him 5 yards deep in the end zone for the score. Purdue had scored 24 points in the second quarter alone and led 34–7. There was entire half of football left, but the game, for all intents and purposes, was over.

For the day, Blough finished 11 of 13 for 235 yards and three scores, while Fuller ran for 146 yards on just sixteen carries, reaching the end zone once. Coach Brohm got win number one, and Boilermaker faithful headed home very happy.

October 7, 2017

Purdue 31, Minnesota 17—Dramatic Win a Fitting Tribute

Standing at 2-2 with Minnesota coming to town, week five of the 2017 season already meant plenty for the Boilermakers. It took on a deeper meaning when, seven days earlier during the team's off week, word reached West Lafayette from the western outpost of Buffalo, Wyoming. The great Joe Tiller had died at the age of seventy-four. Tiller's first team was scheduled to be in attendance for the game with the Gophers, commemorating their twentieth anniversary. That celebration became something more.

A flag that simply read "Joe" flew at the stadium, and both teams honored the coaching legend with helmet stickers. Purdue was energized out of the gate, with the defense forcing a three-and-out to start the game. The offense needed just three plays to get on the board, with quarterback David Blough hitting tight end Cole Herdman for a 20-yard score. The PAT failed and the lead stayed 6–0.

Minnesota answered with a touchdown in the first quarter and another in the second to lead 14–6 at the half. Quarterback Elijah Sindelar led a

Both teams decided on a helmet sticker tribute to one of college football's greatest innovators in the first game played after his untimely passing. *Purdue Athletics.*

scoring drive to open the second half, connecting with D.J. Knox for a 22-yard score to make it 14–13. And that's how it stood through three quarters of play.

Early in the fourth, after a fourth straight Minnesota punt, Sindelar led the offense on a ten-play, 78-yard drive that ended with a short field goal and a 16–14 lead. Just after the kick was converted, Mother Nature decided to have her say. A severe storm swept in from the west and put the game under a weather delay, forcing the entire stadium to be evacuated. Some ninety minutes passed before the teams returned to the field; a fraction of the forty-two thousand fans who had showed up for the opening kick actually returned to their seats. Those who returned saw a finish for the ages.

The Gophers restarted the game with what was basically the perfect drive. Taking possession with just under ten minutes to play on a rain-swamped field, they drove 62 yards on seventeen plays and kicked a field goal to go back on top, 17–16. More importantly, they took seven and a half minutes off the clock, leaving precious little time for the Boilermakers to respond.

Knox took the kickoff at the goal line and found a seam up the near sideline, jump-starting the offense with a return out to the 44-yard line. Markell Jones gained a yard on first down, and Sindelar hit tight end Brycen Hopkins for 6 on second down. Facing third-and-short from midfield, with the clock at 1:33 and running, Sindelar hit Anthony Mahoungou on an

Linebacker Ja'Whaun Bentley put the game on ice with a late pick-six after a thunderstorm drove thousands of fans from the stadium. *Purdue Athletics.*

easy crossing pattern for the first down—except Mahoungou forgot to get tackled, running away from three Gopher defenders all the way to the 12-yard line before being pushed out of bounds.

On the next play, Markell Jones took an inside handoff and bounced it wide right, and then he made a cut he had no business making on a soaking wet field and went untouched into the end zone. Sindelar hit Greg Phillips for a two-point conversion, and the Boilermakers led 24–17 with 1:17 remaining. The Gophers wouldn't go quietly.

It took them just four plays to get into Purdue territory, and on fourth down, with twenty-three seconds to go, Gopher quarterback Conor Rhoda looked for a crossing route to get a first down. He didn't see linebacker Ja'Whaun Bentley, who leaped to make the catch and took off 76 yards the other way for the day's final score.

Sindelar was great in relief of Blough, finishing 19 of 26 for 248 yards and a touchdown. And with Drew Brees, Rosevelt Colvin, Akin Ayodele, Ike Jones and a dozen other members of Tiller's first team in attendance, it gave everyone one more reason to celebrate the legacy of a hugely important member of the Purdue Football family.

November 25, 2017

Purdue 31, Indiana 24—A Bucket and a Bowl to the Winner

The 1967 battle for the Old Oaken Bucket was the most important game in series history, with Indiana taking down no. 3 Purdue to share the Big Ten title with the Boilermakers and earn a trip to the Rose Bowl (that Purdue wasn't eligible for, having gone the previous season). The 2017 edition of the rivalry was nearly as significant, as both teams entered the contest with identical 5-6 records, with the winner ensuring for themselves a postseason trip and the loser going home for the holidays.

A bowl trip would be a wonderful way to end Coach Jeff Brohm's first season in West Lafayette, signaling that the program was far ahead of where most thought possible at the season's outset. Victorious in two of their last three, including a road win at Iowa, the Boilermakers were confident.

Jackson Anthrop got the Boilers on the board early with a 5-yard rushing touchdown, capitalizing on linebacker Garrett Hudson's interception on the Hoosiers' first play from scrimmage. IU answered back with a score late in the first to make it 7–7. Anthrop scored again in the second quarter,

Few Old Oaken Bucket battles have had more on the line than the "Winner goes to a bowl" game in 2017, which saw the Boilermakers come out on top, 31–24. *Purdue Athletics.*

and then, in the final minute of the first half, quarterback Elijah Sindelar connected with receiver Anthony Mahoungou on a 49-yard touchdown pass. The Hoosiers were able to get a last-second field goal to make it 21–10 at the half.

Neither team did much in the third quarter until J.D. Dellinger booted through a short field goal after a long drive to make it 24–10, good guys. Sindelar connected with receiver Isaac Zico early in the fourth quarter to make it 31–10, the game seemingly well in hand. But rivalries are rarely that simple.

Indiana took over with under eight minutes remaining, down three scores. It took less than two minutes to get one of them back. Then IU recovered an onside kick to get the ball right back. Facing real adversity and a bit of shakiness for the first time all day, the Purdue defense responded. After an incomplete pass on first down, linebacker Danny Ezechukwu came up with a huge sack on second down. The Hoosiers gained 10 yards on third down, setting up a fourth-and-6. Ezechukwu made the fourth-down stop as well, and Purdue got the ball back thanks to the turnover on downs.

The offense didn't do much, but it did run over a minute off the clock while forcing Indiana to use its final two timeouts. Indiana scored again with just over a minute to go, but the onside kick failed this time. Sindelar took a knee twice, and the game was over. As fans streamed onto the field to celebrate the win, the players hoisted the Bucket overhead, ending Indiana's four-year winning streak in the series. The Hoosiers handed over the trophy and headed to the offseason, while the Boilermakers were on their way to San Francisco for a classic Foster Farms Bowl win over Arizona.

September 15, 2018

Missouri 40, Purdue 37—So, So Close

After the 2017 season ended with a bang, the 2018 season began with a whimper. A close loss to Northwestern on opening night was followed by an inexplicable loss to Eastern Michigan in a week-two torrential downpour of bad fortune. Next up for the Boilermakers was a motivated Missouri team with a ranked Boston College squad just over the horizon.

Missouri came to Ross-Ade 2-0 on the year, but it was their loss to the Boilermakers a year earlier that motivated the Tigers. Purdue went to Columbia and demolished Mizzou 35–3. It was apparent that the visitors were dialed in from the start this time around. They opened the game with a ten-play drive that ended in a field goal. The Boilermakers responded with a four-play, 86-yard drive, with quarterback David Blough hitting receiver Terry Wright for a 12-yard score.

Mizzou reached the end zone on its third drive and then intercepted Blough on the ensuing possession and turned that into another field goal. It was 13–7 at the end of the first quarter. Mizzou had already compiled 187 yards of offense but settled for two field goals after long drives.

Spencer Evans hit a field goal early in the second quarter to pull Purdue within three, 13–10. Missouri quarterback Drew Lock threw touchdown passes on his team's next two possessions, and midway through the second quarter, Purdue trailed 27–10. Blough put together Purdue's best sustained drive of the day going 75 yards in ten plays with the quarterback diving in for the score to make it 27–17 with under three minutes to go.

Now the defense had to try to keep the Tigers off the board and get to halftime. Missouri calmly drove into field goal range and trotted out the field goal unit with thirty-two seconds remaining. It was a 50-yard attempt, a difficult kick under perfect circumstances and an impossible one if the offensive line leaves a man unblocked. Safety Jacob Thieneman ran through the left side of the Mizzou line untouched and blocked the kick, which teammate Navon Mosely recovered.

With the ball near midfield and thirty-two seconds, Blough hit tight end Brycen Hopkins for 31 yards. After a timeout, Blough dropped back to pass and saw the middle of the field open so he took off on the ground for a 21-yard gain to the 3-yard line. After another timeout, Blough hit Hopkins for a score to make it 27–24 at the half. The teams had combined for more than 700 yards of offense in just thirty minutes.

Purdue tied the game up in the third quarter before Missouri reeled off 10 consecutive points to go up 37–27. Blough connected with receiver Rondale Moore early in the fourth to make it 37–34. The Boilers caught a huge break on the first play of the drive when Blough threw a pass to Markell Jones downfield. Jones was hit immediately, and the ball popped up in the air, where Hopkins grabbed it and rumbled downfield for a 74-yard gain. Moore scored on the next play.

The defense made another stop when cornerback Kenneth Major came up with a red zone interception. Now down 3 with the ball and under eight minutes to go, the feeling in the stadium had certainly turned. Blough calmly drove the Boilermakers 82 yards for a first-and-goal at the Missouri 8-yard line.

Receiver Jared Sparks had the go-ahead touchdown for about three minutes, until replay overturned the call and forced Purdue to kick a field goal to tie Missouri. *Purdue Athletics.*

On third-and-goal, Blough dropped back and threw a perfect fade pass to the left corner of the end zone. Receiver Jared Sparks went up and made the contested catch, landing in bounds for the go-ahead score. Then the referees decided to review the catch and overturned the touchdown, much to the chagrin of forty-eight thousand fans in attendance and the three broadcasters calling the game for the BTN. Evans kicked a field goal on the next play to tie the game 37–37.

Missouri kicked a game-winning field goal as time expired. Despite the outcome and questionable call, fans had reason for hope. Sure, their team was 0-3, with those three losses coming by a total of eight points. But they'd just seen Blough shatter the single-game passing record with 572 yards through the air. They'd seen Moore catch eleven passes for 137 yards in just his third collegiate game, and it was already apparent that he was an emerging superstar. Three different receivers broke the century mark for the first time since 2007. Better days were just ahead.

October 20, 2018

Purdue 49, No. 2 Ohio State 20—The Tyler Trent Game

Following their loss to Missouri, the Boilermakers ripped off three straight wins, taking down no. 23 Boston College and then winning a pair of road games at Nebraska and Illinois. Standing at 3-3 at the season's halfway mark was a fine place to be, but very few people gave the Boilermakers much of a chance against the next opponent, no. 2 Ohio State. Well, except for one extraordinary fan.

This space is insufficient to tell the story of Tyler Trent and his impact on Purdue Football, the university itself or the world beyond West Lafayette. For that story, read *The Upset: Life (Sports), Death and the Legacy We Leave in the Middle*, Tyler's autobiography. In the fall of 2018, Trent was a sophomore at Purdue, a diehard fan of the Boilermakers and in the middle the fight of his life against cancer. He had grown close with the football team, with the captains driving an hour to his Indianapolis-area home following the game at Nebraska to present a game ball and celebrate the triumph.

During the lead-up to the Ohio State game, Tyler would tell anyone who would listen that his Boilermakers were going to pull the upset. With his story featured that morning on ESPN's *College GameDay*, the world had come

Any one of the sixty thousand in attendance will tell you that there was a special feeling in the air on October 20, 2018. *Purdue Athletics.*

to know Tyler. When the game kicked off in prime time on ABC, millions tuned in to see if the young man's prediction would come true.

The teams traded punts for most of the first quarter, but with just over a minute to go in the opening stanza, quarterback David Blough hit receiver Isaac Zico for a 13-yard scoring pass, capping off a 98-yard drive and putting the home team up 7–0.

The Buckeyes drove deep into Purdue territory, but the defense held them to a field goal. The teams traded punts again before Ohio State went on a lengthy drive that came up empty after a missed field goal with less than two minutes remaining in the half. Running back D.J. Knox gained 23 yards on the ground on two running plays to get the ball out near midfield. Blough then hit Zico for a 37-yard gain to the OSU 20-yard line. A pass to Rondale Moore picked up 7, and two incomplete throws brought up fourth down; out came the field goal unit. The snap came to holder Joe Schopper, and as Evans approached the ball, Schopper snatched it back and took off sprinting around the left end. On fourth-and-3, Schopper got 4 yards on the fake field goal, dropping his shoulder and punishing the Buckeye defender who finally brought him down. Blough hit Moore for a touchdown, and the Boilermakers led 14–3 at the break.

The Buckeyes received the ball to start the second half and, after another long drive, had to once again settle for a field goal. Purdue caught a bit of luck when Schopper was taken out after a punt and the roughing the kicker penalty extended the drive. Knox finished off the drive with a short touchdown run, and the home team led 21–6.

The Buckeyes responded with a 73-yard drive that ended 2 yards short of the end zone when quarterback Dwayne Haskins misfired on a fourth-down pass to K.J. Hill. The third quarter ended with the Boilermakers still up 21–6.

The Purdue offense went into ball-control mode when they got it back, with Blough hitting short passes and handing it off plenty. On third-and-9 from just across midfield, Knox took an inside handoff and, 42 yards later, was standing in the end zone for the second time on the day. The crowd of more than sixty thousand was in hysterics as the home team now led 28–6 in the fourth.

The Buckeyes finally reached the end zone to make it 28–13, but Purdue answered right back and again it was Knox. This time, Blough faked the jet sweep handoff to Moore and gave it to Knox up the middle, and D.J. went 40 yards through the middle of the OSU defense, untouched. The Boilermakers led 35–13 with less than seven minutes to go, and the party had begun.

Ohio State scored a second touchdown, but the onside kick failed so the Boilermakers go the ball near midfield. By this time, Tyler and his family had made their way to the sidelines to revel in the victory. As younger brother Ethan pushed his wheelchair up the ramp toward the Purdue locker room, Blough swung a third-down pass to Moore in the left flat. Rondale caught the ball, broke a tackle to reach the first-down marker and then bullied his way through a second would-be tackler, eventually shaking that man free as well. Two more Buckeyes got their hands on Moore, and he ran away from three others on his way to an iconic 43-yard score and a 42–20 lead.

The icing on the cake came on OSU's next possession when linebacker Markus Bailey, a native of Columbus, Ohio, intercepted Haskins and returned it for a touchdown. As the jubilant crowd stormed the field, fireworks exploded in the distance, putting the exclamation point on an upset for the ages.

The Trent family were in the locker room with the team, with hugs all around. In the postgame press conference, Tyler was given a chance to address the media before Coach Jeff Brohm. Prior to that address, David Blough walked up to his friend away from the microphones and leaned in close.

"I love you man," Blough said. "We thought about you every time we took the field."

"Moore in space…a burst of speed, first down for Purdue…HE'S STILL GOING!" Chris Fowler, October 20, 2018. *Purdue Athletics.*

No one had more faith in the Boilermakers upsetting no. 2 Ohio State than Tyler Trent, here with ESPN's Tom Rinaldi. *Purdue Athletics.*

"I love you, too," Trent quietly replied through a weary smile.

It was a poignant moment shared by two young men the sporting world had fallen in love with: one who had just engineered the year's biggest upset and one who had never faltered in his belief that it would happen.

November 3, 2018

Purdue 38, No. 19 Iowa 36—Evans Hands Hawkeyes Heartbreak

A letdown is almost unavoidable following a win the likes of the Purdue upset over Ohio State, and that's exactly what happened in East Lansing the following weekend. After falling to the Spartans, the Boilermakers returned home at 4-4 on the year with a ranked Iowa team coming to town.

Quarterback David Blough connected with Isaac Zico for a 36-yard touchdown on the game's opening drive, and the Hawkeyes responded with a score of their own to make it 7–7. Purdue retook the lead on a short Markell Jones touchdown run late in the first quarter.

The Hawkeyes opened the second quarter with a field goal, and then Blough found receiver Terry Wright on a 41-yard touchdown pass that made it 21–10. The Hawkeyes got a touchdown late in the first half, helped by 30 free yards thanks to a questionable kick-catch interference call and an unsportsmanlike conduct penalty against an assistant coach after the play, so the score was 21–17 at the break.

The defense opened the second half by forcing a quick three-and-out, and Blough put together an even quicker scoring drive. One play for 82 yards and the senior quarterback connected with Wright for a long touchdown extending the lead to 28–17.

Iowa answered with a five-play, 81-yard touchdown drive, but Blough and Wright hooked up for a third score near the end of the quarter; Purdue took a 35–23 lead into the fourth. A pair of rushing touchdowns by Mekhi Sargent gave the Hawkeyes the lead for the first time all day, 36–35, with ten minutes to play. The teams traded punts, and with four and a half minutes to go, the Boilermakers got the ball back at midfield for what would likely be their final possession.

Jones started with a 12-yard rush, but three subsequent running plays totaled just 8 yards, bringing up a fourth-and-2, just outside the range of kicker Spencer Evans. Blough took the shotgun snap and sprinted left on

Kicker Spencer Evans puts the finishing touch on the team's third ranked win of the 2018 season. *Purdue Athletics.*

a quarterback sweep, gaining 7 yards and securing the first down with two minutes to play. A holding call set the Boilermakers back 10 yards, but Purdue got that back and more on a defensive pass interference call two plays later.

Now well inside Evans's comfortable range, a safe handoff was called for D.J. Knox, who proceeded to gain 11 yards down to the 5-yard line. Three plays later, after bleeding the clock all the way down, Evans drilled the game winner from 25 yards out to give the Boilermakers their third win over a ranked opponent on the season, the first time that had happened since 2003. While Evans may have been the hero, Terry Wright was the star of the day, catching six passes for 146 yards and three touchdowns.

September 7, 2019

Purdue 42, Vanderbilt 24—Sindelar Lights Up Vandy

On January 1, 2019, Tyler Trent lost his battle with cancer, less than a week after he had joined his Boilermaker brothers at the Music City Bowl in

Nashville. Shortly after his passing, the program announced that it would be dedicating the student ticket gate at Ross-Ade Stadium in his honor in a ceremony before the home opener in the fall of 2019. The day had added significance to the Trent family, as it represented what would have been Tyler's twenty-first birthday.

Two hours before the game, the Tyler Trent Student Entrance was dedicated, with the Trent family and several university officials in attendance. At kickoff, it was clear to the more than fifty thousand in attendance, given the significance of the day, that this was a game Purdue wouldn't lose. That feeling was bolstered after the first quarter when the crowd sang "Happy Birthday" to Tyler.

Quarterback Elijah Sindelar was spectacular. He completed 34 of 52 for 509 yards and five scores while running for a sixth late in the game. He became the sixth Purdue quarterback to surpass 500 yards in a game, but he wasn't the only star of the day. Sophomore receiver Rondale Moore grabbed thirteen passes for 220 yards and a score, while senior tight end Brycen Hopkins found the end zone twice.

The win over Vanderbilt gave Purdue just its second victory over a Southeastern Conference opponent since 1979. It was a much-needed win after the team had stubbed its toe in the season opener a week earlier at Nevada and suggested that the program was on the right trajectory.

November 2, 2019

Purdue 31, Nebraska 27—O'Connell Perfect in Relief

The 2019 season went sideways for the Boilermakers on a single play in the first quarter of the week four game against Minnesota when starting quarterback Elijah Sindelar and All-American receiver Rondale Moore were both lost for the season. The team nearly rallied to win that game and defeated Maryland handily two weeks later, but the record stood at 2-6 when Nebraska came to town.

The Huskers were expected to contend in the Big Ten West under second-year head coach Scott Frost, but they arrived in West Lafayette at 4-4 on the year after losing their last two. Nebraska jumped out to a 10–0 lead before a pair of Jack Plummer touchdown passes gave the home team the halftime lead. The first scoring drive covered 89 yards on ten plays, with Plummer hitting running back King Doerue for the score. The second drive went

96 yards on twelve plays, with Plummer connecting with tight end Payne Durham for the score with just seven seconds remaining in the half.

Plummer, a redshirt freshman, had been very good in the month since taking over for the injured Sindelar. He'd completed 60 percent of his passes for nearly 1,100 yards and eight touchdowns with four interceptions. His steady hand had the Boilermakers on top at the break. The teams traded field goals in the third quarter and headed to the final fifteen minutes with Purdue up 17–13.

Nebraska went on top early in the fourth quarter with a rushing touchdown by quarterback Adrian Martinez. Plummer came back out and led the Boilermakers down the field once more. He scrambled for a 14-yard gain to the eighth play of the drive but went down awkwardly and got up limping on a broken ankle. Enter walk-on quarterback Aidan O'Connell.

The Boilermakers made it easy on the new quarterback as he handed off three times to Doerue, and the running back did the rest, scoring on a 7-yard run to put Purdue back on top, 24–20, with just under seven minutes to go. The Huskers responded with another drive that ended in a rushing touchdown for Martinez and took the lead, 27–24, with just over four minutes to play.

Former walk-on quarterback Aidan O'Connell was nearly perfect in late relief against Nebraska. *Purdue Athletics.*

On the ensuing drive, O'Connell hit Durham for a 7-yard gain on first down, and Doerue picked up 2 on the next play. O'Connell ran a QB sneak on the next snap and got a new set of downs. He then completed four straight passes, the last one a 26-yard gain to tight end Brycen Hopkins. Doerue ran for 3 more yards to the Nebraska 24-yard line as the clock continued to run with less than two minutes to go. Another completion to Hopkins gained 10 yards, and then Doerue gained 5 yards on two carries, setting up a third-down from the Nebraska 9-yard line.

A field goal would tie it, so there was no need to take any chances. Receiver Milton Wright came in pre-snap motion from his wide-left position, and at the snap the entire offense flowed to the right, selling the jet sweep. The entire defense flowed that direction as well, so they missed that receiver David Bell had done the opposite at the snap, sweeping left from his near-right receiver position. Bell took the handoff from O'Connell and strolled in untouched from 9 yards out, giving the Boilermakers the 27–24 win.

Before going down with his fourth-quarter injury, Plummer had thrown for 242 yards and a pair of touchdowns while rushing for another 61 yards. When O'Connell came in, the offense didn't miss a beat. The former third-string quarterback completed all five passes he attempted for 62 yards on the game-winning drive.

2020s
OVERCOMING ADVERSITY

O'CONNELL, BELL AND COVID-19

OCTOBER 24, 2020

PURDUE 24, IOWA 20—A SEASON OPENER LIKE NO OTHER

The 2020 College Football season stands alone as the strangest year in the sport's history. With the country in the throes of a global pandemic due to the COVID-19 outbreak, the season began with fall training camp and then was suspended in mid-August. A little more than a month later, the Big Ten conference announced an eight-game, conference-only schedule to begin in late October, with the caveat that safety measures would be taken for all participants and no fans would be allowed in the stadiums beyond family members of the participants.

So it was that the 2020 season opener against Iowa kicked off on October 24 in front of fewer than one thousand people. The teams took the field to the sounds of artificial crowd noise with none of the pomp and circumstance that has come to define the college football game day experience over the decades. No All-American Marching Band regaling everyone with "Hail Purdue!" No "I Am an American." No fly-overs or sky divers or special game ball deliveries. Only football. And the fans at home watching along on the B1G Network were glad to have it.

Among those watching the game from home was Head Coach Jeff Brohm. The head man had tested positive for COVID-19 earlier in the week and was quarantining in the basement of his home less than a mile from

With games played in an empty stadium during the 2020 season, unique measures were taken to make it seem as normal as possible, with famous faces in the "crowd." *Purdue Athletics.*

Ross-Ade Stadium. Offensive coordinator Brian Brohm would be leading the team onto the field on this most strange day.

David Bell got the Boilermakers on the board on a 9-yard touchdown pass from Aidan O'Connell midway through the first quarter. The sophomore receiver was already someone Hawkeye fans were weary of as he had thirteen catches for 197 yards and a touchdown against them his freshman year. He was just getting started.

The Hawkeyes scored twice in the second quarter to go up 14–7, but the Boilermakers drove 75 yards to tie the game up on another O'Connell-to-Bell pass. Iowa kicked a short field goal as time expired in the first half to make it 17–14 at the break.

The teams traded punts in a scoreless third quarter, and the Hawks extended their lead early in the fourth with another short field goal. Kicker J.D. Dellinger got 3 points back with a 29-yard field goal of his own, capping off a 71-yard drive by the Boilermakers. Up 20–17 with the ball and less than eight minutes to go, the Hawkeyes focused on ball control and running the clock down. After passing for a first down, three straight rushes by Iowa running back Mekhi Sargent gained 37 yards and got the Hawks into Purdue territory. However, on the third rushing play, cornerback Dedrick Mackey dove and ripped the ball loose, while teammate Cam Allen recovered the fumble.

The offense took over now, down three, for what might be their final possession of the day. An incomplete first-down pass and a short run by Zander Horvath set up third-and-5. O'Connell hit Bell on a short crossing pattern, and the receiver snaked his way forward for a 10-yard gain. Horvath then gained 9 yards, getting the ball out across midfield, but went backward on the next snap to set up another third down. This time the Boilermakers kept it on the ground, and Horvath got just enough for a new set of downs.

O'Connell hit Milton Wright for a first down, and then the Boilermakers caught a break as an Iowa defender grabbed Aidan's facemask while attempting a sack. Purdue took the 15 penalty yards and had a fresh set of downs at the Iowa 22-yard line. Horvath gained 16 yards on two carries, giving him 129 rushing yards on the day. O'Connell then dropped back and threw a pass over the head of a wide-open Bell to bring up yet another third down.

Fans or no fans, receiver David Bell was a star against the Hawkeyes, with thirteen catches for 121 yards and three scores, including the game winner. *Purdue Athletics.*

Horvath went in motion, emptying the backfield and pulling the Iowa safety away from Bell, who had lined up in the slot on the right. An Iowa linebacker drifted out to try covering the future All-American but was far too little, far too late. O'Connell's pass was perfect this time as the pair connected for their third score on the afternoon.

The Boilermakers took the opener 24–20, with Bell grabbing thirteen receptions for 121 yards and all three touchdowns. The Boilermakers beat Illinois in week two and then had the game against Wisconsin canceled due to COVID before losing four in a row. The final week of the season was canceled as well due to the virus, meaning the Old Oaken Bucket game wouldn't happen for the first time in nearly a century. While the fans were overjoyed to have football to watch, there was a sense of relief once the season was over that hopefully they would never have to witness those circumstances again.

September 4, 2021

Purdue 30, Oregon State 21—Welcome Back to Ross-Ade Stadium!

By September 2021, the global pandemic still hadn't come to an end, but the world had slowly begun to return to normal. For anyone who was within earshot of Ross-Ade Stadium on the evening of September 4, one thing was undeniable: college football was back! A misty rain and overcast skies did nothing to dampen the mood of nearly fifty-four thousand Boilermaker faithful who packed the stands.

For the first time in nearly two years, they cheered. They cheered for the All-American Marching Band. They cheered for Cradle of Quarterbacks member Jim Everett, in from L.A. for the occasion. They cheered for the men's basketball team, honored on the field early in the evening. But they cheered loudest for the Boilermaker football team. And they had plenty to cheer for.

Oregon State got on the board first with a short rushing touchdown, but Zander Horvath answered with a rushing score of his own and the first quarter ended in a deadlock, 7–7. Graduate transfer kicker Mitchell Fineran drilled two field goals in the second quarter, including a 49-yarder, to put Purdue up 13–7 at the break.

Fineran struck again in the third quarter, extending the lead to 16–7 in favor of the home team, but the Beavers pulled to within 2 early in the

The 2021 home opener had an electric atmosphere, as fifty-four thousand fans welcomed the Boilermakers back to the field after a long, strange year away. *Purdue Athletics.*

fourth quarter. A long drive ended with a short touchdown run making it 16–14. The Boilermakers went nowhere and had to punt. On the ensuing possession, Oregon State had a fourth-and-2 from their own 39-yard line and decided to go for it. With eight minutes to go, the Beavers were trying to create some momentum. Cornerback Cory Trice had other ideas. A play-action pass got the Oregon State receiver single coverage, and quarterback Chance Nolan lofted a perfect pass 35 yards downfield. Trice used great closing speed and every inch of his six-foot-two frame to perfectly knock the ball away and force the turnover on downs.

Three Horvath runs and three Plummer passes to tight end Payne Durham led the Boilermakers to a 23–14 lead with Durham getting his first score of the day. The Beavers answered back with a score in less than two minutes, making it 23–21 with just over three minutes to go. Purdue took the field just needing to control the ball and run the clock down. Instead, Plummer hit David Bell for a 22-yard gain on first down. A pair of short plays forced Oregon State to use two timeouts and brought up third-and-2 from the 50-yard line.

Knowing that the Boilermakers needed 2 yards to essentially end the game, Oregon State had all eleven defenders within 5 yards of the line of

Those in attendance saw a great game against Oregon State, with the home team coming out on top, 30–21. *Purdue Athletics.*

scrimmage. At the snap, the defense surged forward as Plummer dropped back and faked a handoff to Horvath. Durham acted as if he was looking to pick up a block on the second level and then just ran past everyone so when Plummer lofted a pass to him 10 yards downfield, he was all alone. Durham grabbed the ball and strolled into the end zone for the 50-yard score.

On the game, Plummer finished 29 of 41 for 313 yards and two scores, while Bell and Durham went over 100 yards on the day receiving. The stadium was electric, the atmosphere unforgettable. It was wonderful that the Boilermakers won, but the result really mattered far less than the event itself. College football was back, and for three hours every Saturday in the fall, that mattered more than most could express through words.

NOVEMBER 6, 2021

PURDUE 40, NO. 3 MICHIGAN STATE 29—O'CONNELL, BELL SMASH SPARTANS

The win over Oregon State was a good one to open the season, but the college football world sat up and took notice of the Boilermakers in mid-October when they went into Iowa City and dominated no. 2 Iowa. The

Boilermakers lost some momentum when they fell to Wisconsin a week later but got their swagger back with a win at Nebraska to improve to 5-3 on the year with an undefeated Michigan State coming to town.

The Spartans were ranked no. 3 and had just beaten no. 6 Michigan. Nearly fifty-eight thousand turned out on the crisp November afternoon, and they saw their Boilermakers get on the board early with a touchdown pass from Aidan O'Connell to David Bell. The Spartans tied it up on their next possession, and the game headed to the second quarter 7–7. O'Connell connected with receiver Broc Thompson early in the second quarter to put Purdue up 14–7 and then hit receiver Jackson Anthrop for a 39-yard score to make it 21–7. Spartan running back Kenneth Walker, a Heisman Trophy frontrunner, made it 21–14 at the half with a late touchdown run.

The Spartans tied it at 21-21 with a quick strike touchdown after a Purdue fumble. Purdue responded with a 70-yard scoring drive with running back King Doerue plunging in from the 1-yard line. After forcing a Spartan punt, it was once again David Bell's time to shine. On third-and-9, O'Connell hit the receiver on a go-route along the right sideline. Bell went up to catch the ball and landed with both feet in bounds 28 yards downfield. He then somehow harnessed all of his momentum to a complete stop and shrugged off an MSU defender, maintained possession of the ball and kept his toes in bounds. Then he took off sprinting for another 22 yards before being brought down.

The drive ended with a Mitchell Fineran field goal to put the home team up 31–21. It could've been more, but O'Connell, in a rare misfire on the day, sailed one over the head of slot receiver T.J. Sheffield in the end zone. The Spartans, now desperate to stay in a game that seemed to be slipping away, went three-and-out on their next possession. Fineran added a field goal on Purdue's next possession to make it 34–21. MSU was moving the ball on its next drive, but it came crashing to a halt when cornerback Dedrick Mackey made a perfect play on a fourth-down pass. In one-on-one coverage on the outside, Mackey stayed on the inside shoulder of his receiver and then got a great break on a pass near the pylon, diving for the interception. The defense had risen to the challenge once more.

Starting on the 1-yard line, O'Connell did the safest thing he knew how to do. He found David Bell for a 17-yard back-shoulder pass. After a few short runs and a pass to Horvath, O'Connell hit Bell again for a 53-yard gain. Four plays later, Fineran kicked his third field goal of the half to put Purdue up 37–21.

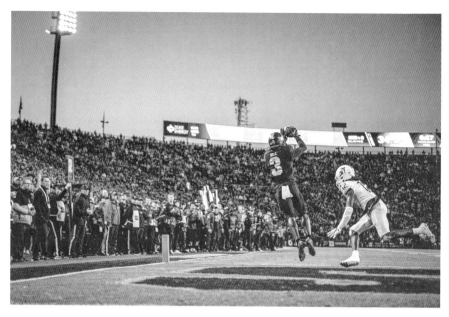

Receiver David Bell was otherworldly in the upset against no. 3 Michigan State—eleven catches, 217 yards and this toe-tapping touchdown. *Purdue Athletics.*

Fans swarm the field following the upset of the Spartans, the second win over a Top 3 team of the 2021 season and the program's fifteenth overall. *Purdue Athletics.*

Michigan State scored quickly and converted a two-point try to make it an eight-point game with five minutes to play. But they simply couldn't stop the Boilermaker offense. On first down, O'Connell dropped back and hit Doerue on a screen pass. The running back settled in behind a wall of blockers and rumbled 46 yards into MSU territory. O'Connell then hit Milton Wright for a key third-down conversion, and the clock kept rolling. A completion to Jackson Anthrop and four Doerue run plays brought the clock under a minute, and when Fineran hit his fourth field goal of the game, the upset was complete.

Fans stormed the field at the final whistle as their Boilermakers had secured a second win over a team ranked in the Top 3 of the AP Poll for the first time since 1960. On the day, O'Connell finished 40 of 54 for 536 yards and three touchdowns, while Bell finished with eleven catches for 217 yards and a score. The defense gave up just two scores in MSU's four trips to the red zone while forcing two turnovers.

The Boilermakers fell to Ohio State the following week but closed the season on a three-game winning streak, including a thrilling TransPerfect Music City Bowl win over Tennessee to secure a 9-4 record, the first nine-win season for the program since 2003.

November 25, 2023

Purdue 35, Indiana 31—A New Era Dawns

Fresh off the program's first appearance in the Big Ten Championship game and an appearance in the Cheez-It Citrus Bowl, the reset button was once again pushed in West Lafayette. When Head Coach Jeff Brohm left for his alma mater, Ryan Walters stepped in to take over the program.

The first-time head coach's inaugural season also saw a brand-new look for the historic stadium. Additions to the stadium included closing in the south end zone with a permanent structure for the first time. And the team would enter the field through the new Tiller Tunnel, a tribute to the great Joe Tiller.

Sell-out crowds filled Ross-Ade all season long, although a daunting schedule led to their beloved Boilermakers entering the Bucket game with a 3-8 record. Still, nearly sixty thousand people showed up on a chilly afternoon, and they were treated to a thriller.

Coach Ryan Walters leads the team out of Tiller Tunnel during the 2023 season. *Purdue Athletics.*

Indiana took a 7–0 lead in the first quarter, but quarterback Hudson Card tied it up early in the second, hitting tight end George Burhenn for a score. Indiana responded right away to go up 14–6 and were looking for more when an interception by freshman safety Dillon Thieneman snuffed out a drive. Card led a twelve-play, 78-yard drive in under three minutes to make the score 14–12 at the break.

The Boilermakers took a 15–14 lead on the opening drive of the second half, but their joy was short-lived. IU returned the ensuing kickoff 100 yards to go back on top. Ben Freehill added a second field goal to cut the lead to 21–18, but the visitors scored another touchdown late in the third quarter to take a 10-point lead.

The first play of the fourth quarter found Purdue facing a fourth-and-2. With the outcome of the game possibly riding on the result of this one snap, Card faked a quarterback draw and then sailed a perfect pass over the top of the IU defense to running back Devin Mockobee. The sophomore did the rest, sprinting 38 yards to pay dirt, cutting the lead to 28–25.

Freehill tied it up with a 35-yard field goal, but Indiana responded with a field goal of its own and took the lead back with five minutes remaining. On first down, Card hit Deion Burks for a 44-yard gain, with the sophomore receiver making a spectacular diving catch. A short Mockobee rush and a 14-yard pass to Burks made it first-and-goal at the 6. After a Mockobee rush lost 4 yards, Card called his own number. A quarterback draw straight up the middle, a quick cut left and a great block by Mockobee found Card in the end zone for the winning score as the Boilers retained the Old Oaken Bucket for a third straight year.

Fans streamed out of Ross-Ade Stadium happy with the outcome and hopeful for the future. They had a coach and a quarterback and wonderful new look to their historic stadium. This vaunted home of the Boilermakers, the place where countless memories had been born over the past century, was now primed to continue making people fall in love with Purdue University for decades to come.

ABOUT THE AUTHOR

Cory Palm has worked in and around college football for nearly two decades, although he's been immersed in the sport for nearly his whole life. He is currently the director of broadcast services for Purdue Athletics, helping to tell the stories of current student-athletes in partnership with the B1G Network. After studying broadcast journalism at Michigan State University, Cory attained his MA degree in public relations and sport management from Purdue in 2008. His previously published works include *Perfect Warriors: Touchdown Tony Butkovich and the 1943 Purdue Football Team*, the story of Purdue's undefeated team from the World War II era. Cory also directed and produced a companion documentary on that team that aired to acclaim on the B1G Network. Cory has also published a children's book he coauthored with his daughter, Alyssa. Having lived all across the Midwest, Cory; his wife, Jaclyn; and their daughter, Alyssa, now call Lafayette, Indiana, home.

Visit us at
www.historypress.com